ENGAGING Children with MUSIC

Second Edition

A Handbook for Elementary Teachers

CORA BIGWOOD
ANNA LANGLEY
LAURA MCGREGOR

Kendall Hunt
publishing company

DEDICATION

I would like to extend my gratitude to University of Houston's Moores School of Music, the Music Education department and the School of Education for giving me the opportunity to do what I love and to David Bigwood for his technical support and encouragement.

Cora Morgan Bigwood
BM University of Houston
MM New England Conservatory

Many thanks to my friends and colleagues who inspired me through music. I appreciate your creativeness, dedication and passion for what you do.

Anna Langley
BS Music Capital University
MEd Sam Houston State University

A grateful Thank you to all my family, friends, music teachers, and students who have encouraged me and challenged me to share the joy of music all my life! "Blessings all mine, with 10,000 beside."

Laura McGregor
BA Baylor University
MEd Texas A&M University

CONTENTS

FOREWORD, INTRODUCTION

Our three goals in writing this book were to:

- Provide a useful, practical musical background and resource enabling classroom teachers to comfortably integrate music into their lessons.
- Introduce and provide a foundation and working knowledge of the music elements.
- Provide an engaging resource of materials using the musical elements.

Dear Educator,

Music can provide the foundation for a lifelong journey of education and personal development. You have the opportunity to support this foundation for every student you encounter. You may be their first informal music teacher.

As teachers, it is our duty to see that our students receive a solid foundation in all areas of study. In music this is often based on traditional folk songs, dances, movement, instrument playing, and listening to the classics as well as world music. They not only can learn the formal structure of music, but also how to improvise and create new ideas, and grow in confidence. Through music they learn to think as individuals and to work in groups—life skills in today's world.

We are fortunate to live in a time where music is accessible to all in a variety of forms: acoustic, electronic, digital—live and recorded. We have the opportunity to influence the performers and audiences of tomorrow. This is a very exciting thought.

Your classroom will be unique. Schedules, class size and support may vary within a school and perhaps throughout the district. The student population, district budgets and policies, local, state and national standards will interact to require that you develop a teaching plan that works for you. Our goal is to provide you with the musical knowledge and skills to help achieve these standards.

We applaud your willingness to learn new material and hope that you will encourage others to do so. We wish you much success in using this handbook and **engaging your students with music** in a foundation of learning. Thank you for your support to the education of your future students.

Cora Bigwood, Anna Langley, Laura McGregor

ENGAGING THE FOUNDATION— MUSIC AND YOU

WHAT IS MUSIC?

We hear music all around us. It is a part of our lives whether it is in the background or what we choose to listen to as we are relaxing or working. It creates a common bond and experience for celebrations and other special occasions. Music can invoke memories, motivate and heal us. Music is an art form and a part of our culture and heritage.

One definition of music is sound organized in time. There are common threads of elements labeled: rhythm, melody, harmony, expression, timbre, texture, and form. These elements remain constant in music, yet music itself is always changing. We will be working with these elements and discovering what it is that draws us in to a specific selection of music.

HOW DO WE LISTEN TO MUSIC AND WHAT ARE WE HEARING?

What appeals to you as a listener? What are the things you hear and how do they relate to each other? Is it:

- the unique sound quality (timbre) of the voice or instruments you hear?
- how many voices or instruments and how they relate to each other?
- a catchy rhythm pattern?
- how the music makes you feel?
- the lyrics and their message?
- how expressive the music is—loud or soft? fast or slow?

When you listen to music, the creative combinations of the elements of music provide you with an interactive experience.

LISTENING ACTIVITY

Thank you to Dr. Julie Kastner for sharing this music activity.

Let your instructor guide you through the following activity as you experiment with what you are hearing. Discuss each part and how it adds to the music in the activity.

Choose a song such as "Best Day of My Life" by American Authors,
https://www.youtube.com/watch?v=Y66j_BUCBMY

TIP BOX

Here are other choices that could be used for a similar activity.

• In the Hall of the Mountain King" by Edvard Grieg

• "Can't Stop the Feeling" from the movie, "Trolls" by Justin Timberlake

• "Happy" by Pharrell Williams

• "Bugler's Holiday" by Leroy Anderson

• Listen for a repeated rhythmic pattern. Clap the pattern: ♩. ♪ ♩ ♩ Add drums to this pattern.

• Do you hear the background singers? Add your voices singing the notes A A F# E D A, or "Sol, Sol Mi Re Do So" on "Oo, oo, oo, oo oo oo".

• Is there an accompaniment? Yes – let's add some of our own using the xylophones. You will be playing the notes D E "Do Re" for 8 beats, changing to B D "La Do" for 8 beats and repeat this pattern.

• Add a group that will sing the lyrics, (these can be found on the internet) and start at the beginning to perform with the music.

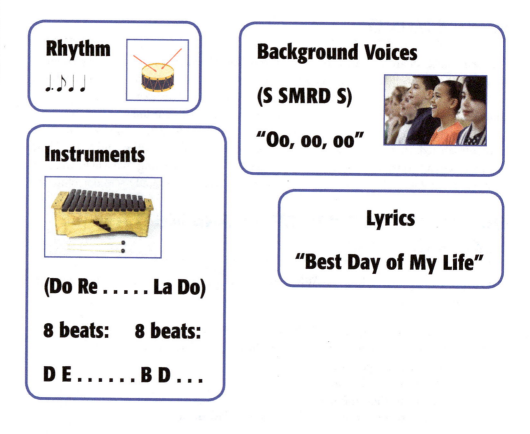

HOW IS MUSIC IMPORTANT?

Let's take a look at what research has to say about music and its value to us.

• You will be placed in a group in class to read and discuss various articles on the value of music education. Report to the class the most important points in your article.

• You will need to reference and apply this information in a later assignment.

Suggested websites:

• Arts Education Partnership

https://www.ecs.org/wp-content/uploads/Music-Matters-1.pdf

• PBS International, The Musical Brain

http://pbsinternational.org/programs/musical-brain-the/

- Southwestern Musician magazine

https://www.tmea.org/resources/southwestern-musician/interactive

- Texas Music Educators Association TMEA

https://www.tmea.org/

HOW WILL YOU USE MUSIC IN YOUR CLASSROOM?

1. Integrate music with other curriculum subjects: Use specific chants and or songs pertaining to your instructional objective or as a review and summary of what you are teaching. Have students create chants to enable the children to use their creativity and retain information.
2. Early morning routines: Start your school day by singing a patriotic song after saying the pledge each morning, calendar time songs and seasonal songs.
3. Transition times: Play a specific song on the recorder that signals, "Clean up, put away and line up to leave the classroom." Suggestion: "Yankee Doodle" or any march style melody.
4. Music signals: Play a finger cymbal or ring a bell as another signal—perhaps meaning, "10 minutes before clean up, or move to the next station, etc."; Clap a rhythmic pattern for the class to echo. When hearing this signal, the class stops what they are doing and listens for directions.
5. Provide a "Brain Break" during instructional time: Do an active rhythmic or music game activity or "break out" dance.
6. Build enthusiasm for Testing days: Have children write simple rhyming chants describing tips for being successful. Perform for their class.
7. Kick off to a Good Year: Rewrite the words to the Black Eyed Peas "I Got A Feeling" song with positive words about having a good year at school. Include your school name or initials and have the school sing along. Add choreography for fun.
8. Music games: Play fun music games for rainy day recess indoors. See Chapter 7 for ideas and game directions.

Brainstorm additional ideas.

9. _____
10. _____

EDUCATIONAL LEARNING THEORISTS

Reflect and write the main idea and importance to your teaching for each of the following theorists.

Jerome Bruner (1915–2016)   was an American psychologist who made significant contributions to human cognitive psychology and cognitive learning theory in educational psychology coining the term "scaffolding." Scaffolding theory identifies the importance of providing students with enough support in the initial stages of learning a new subject. The idea that students should be active in the learning process is known as constructivism. Bruner's idea of a constructivist approach is called the spiral curriculum.

_____
_____
_____

Jean Piaget (1896–1980) was a Swiss psychologist and epistemologist known for his pioneering work in child development. Piaget's theory of cognitive development and epistemological view are together called "genetic epistemology."

Piaget was the first psychologist to make a systematic study of children's cognitive development. His theory included four distinct stages of development: The sensorimotor stage, from birth to age 2. The preoperational stage, from age 2 to about age 7. The concrete operational stage, from age 7 to 11, and formal operational stage. The goal of Piaget's theory is to explain the mechanisms and processes by which the infant, and then the child, develops into an individual who can reason and think using hypotheses.

_____

_____

_____

Abraham Maslow (1908–1970) was an American psychologist who was best known for creating Maslow's hierarchy of needs, a theory of psychological health predicated on fulfilling innate human needs in priority, culminating in self-actualization. This hierarchy of needs is a motivational theory in psychology comprising a five-tier model of human needs, often depicted as hierarchical levels within a pyramid. People are motivated to achieve certain needs and that some needs take precedence over others.

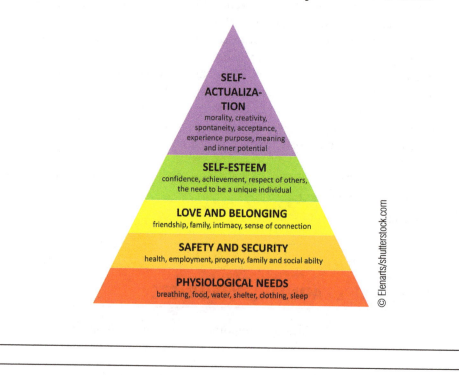

© Elenarts/shutterstock.com

_____

_____

_____

Benjamin Samuel Bloom (1913–1999) was an American educational psychologist who made contributions to the classification of educational objectives and to the theory of mastery learning. Bloom's taxonomy is a set of three hierarchical models used to classify educational learning objectives into levels of complexity and specificity in cognitive, affective, and sensory domains. The cognitive domain list has been the primary focus of most traditional education and is frequently used to structure curriculum learning objectives, assessments, and activities.

create

evaluate

analyze

apply

understand

remember

Bloom's Taxonomy

© mypokcik/shutterstock.com

_____

_____

_____

Howard Earl Gardner (1943–)   is an American developmental psychologist and the John H. and Elisabeth A. Hobbs Professor of Cognition and Education at the Harvard Graduate School of Education at Harvard University. Gardner's theory of multiple intelligences, developed in 1983, suggests that the traditional notion of intelligence, based on I.Q. testing, is far too limited. **These Intelligence modalities are:**

- Musical—rhythmic and harmonic
- Visual—spatial
- Verbal—linguistic
- Logical—mathematical
- Bodily—kinesthetic
- Interpersonal
- Intrapersonal
- Naturalistic

_____

_____

_____

© artellia/shutterstock.com

Lowell Mason (1792–1872) the father of public school music education in America, was born in Medfield, MA on January 8, 1792 into a musical family. Mason composed over 1600 hymn tunes and arranged many others. Aside from composing hymns he was a music publisher and one of the founders of public school music education in the United States. Before this, music education in America consisted mostly of private lessons or singing in church.

_____

_____

_____

MUSIC EDUCATION PHILOSOPHIES

Circle the key words for each education philosophy.

Dalcroze (Jacques Emile-Dalcroze 1865–1950) musical education is based on movement, rhythm, dynamics, tone and form. There are three areas: eurhythmics, solfege, and improvisation. For children, these three areas are integrated into one lesson and later separated as the students become more advanced.

The Gordon Institute for Music Learning is based on extensive research and practical field findings by Edwin E. Gordon and others. Music Learning Theory (MLT) incorporates audiation, Gordon's term for hearing music in the mind with understanding. MLT methods provide teachers with tools to establish sequential curricular objectives to coincide with their own teaching styles and beliefs.

Zoltán Kodály (1882–1967) Hungarian composer, musician, and folk song collector, taught that music is meant to develop the whole being—personally, intellectually and emotionally— "a spiritual food for everybody." Kodály believed that music was a part of everyone's basic heritage and should be started as early as possible.

Kodály methods of teaching are based on the thorough understanding of the concept studied by using musical tools (such as solfege singing) and activities to strengthen the child's ability to grasp the concept. The teacher must be flexible during the teaching process, using tools and aids to enable every learner to be musically literate. Music lessons should bring joy to the student and instill a desire for music that will last a lifetime.

The Orff Approach is based on the ancient Greek concept of music, theatre, and dance being intertwined in which one discipline is not thought of in a solitary manner but is meshed with the others. Twentieth-century German composer Carl Orff (1895–1982) and his collaborator Gunild Keetman (1904–1990) brought back to life this Greek perception of music being fused with drama and dance.

Orff and Keetman composed music to be sung, played, dramatized, improvised, and danced. In Orff teacher-training courses, participants work with language, folk tales, rhymes, and songs in free and metric forms. In Orff Schulwerk, Schulwerk means schooling (in music) through working via participation and student input in the lesson. Children approach music making in a primal "elemental" way that is easily understood in which the child intuitively responds to rhythm and movement. It speaks to the child in a language that he or she understands. This creative process is enhanced with special child sized instruments such as xylophones, metallophones and glockenspiels that are referred to as Orff instruments.

FAME the Feierabend Association for Music Education was founded in 2012 to celebrate and share the unique teachings of Dr. John Feierabend with a wider audience of music educators.

MUSIC ELEMENTS

Vocabulary

Rhythm—A steady *beat* is the constant, underlying, unchanging pulse. *Rhythm* is the duration of sounds and silences in relation to the underlying beat.

Melody—A musical sentence of pitches that can move up, down, have steps, have skips, and can have repeating notes, which creates a "tune" or song when combined with rhythm.

Timbre—The unique tone color and character of an individual voice or musical sound.

Expressive—Nuances in the music, such as dynamics and tempo, that make the music come alive.

Texture—How rhythm, melody and harmony combine to create layers in the music. A thin *texture* contains fewer instruments/voices, whereas a thicker texture would have more instruments/voices.

Harmony—The combination of multiple musical pitches sounding simultaneously.

Form—The overall structure or plan of a piece of music, usually organized in sections.

Value of Music Assignment

VALUE OF MUSIC—Visit websites that discuss the latest music research. Other videos and articles may be suggested in class. Describe, analyze, and evaluate your personal response to all that was discussed and what you have read in an essay.

© oliveromg/Shutterstock.com

CONCLUSION

After reviewing basic educational theories, music elements and research on music, you now have a foundation to begin teaching music to children. A multi-sensory teaching style will allow the learner to use as many senses as possible (tactile-kinesthetic, auditory, visual) to engage multiple parts of the brain. Making music does this naturally. The following chapters will develop rhythm and melody skills through singing, playing instruments, listening and movement.

ENGAGING CHILDREN WITH RHYTHM

CHAPTER 2

Chapter Objectives

After completing this chapter, you will be able to:

- Show the steady pulse in music.
- Know the difference between beat and rhythm.
- Read and write basic rhythms using stick notation/standard notation.
- Play a rhythm game.

Vocabulary

Steady beat—The constant, underlying, unchanging pulse.

Rhythm—The duration of sounds and silences in relation to the underlying beat.

Notation—A universal system of symbols written to represent the sounds and silences of music.

Locomotor movement—Movement done while traveling through shared space.

Nonlocomotor movement—Movement that does not move through space, movement is done in place.

Skill Development
EXPERIENCES WITH STEADY BEAT

1. Walking to a steady beat.
   - Play a song with a strong pulse.
   - Students march in a circle, keeping the beat of the music in their feet,
   - Say, "Beat, Beat, in your feet!" to remind them of their objective.

Extension: Students change to other locomotor movements.

LOCOMOTOR MOVEMENT	
• Walk	• Gallop
• Tip-toe	• Skip
• March	• Side-close
• Stomp	• Slide
• Run	• Jog

2. Use instrumental music that has a steady, strong beat such as "Korobushka" a Russian Folk melody or "The Imperial March" by John Williams.

Variations: Students pretend to drive, using paper plates as a steering wheel.
Extension: Students change to other locomotor movements.

3. Motions with the Beat
   - Choose one of the following selections of music:
     "William Tell Overture: Finale" by Gioachino Rossini
     "Maple Leaf Rag" by Scott Joplin
     "The Thunderer" by John Philip Sousa
     "Raiders of the Lost Ark March" by John Williams
     "Can't Stop the Feeling!" by Justin Timberlake
     "Happy" by Pharrell Williams
   - Teacher places each of the nonlocomotor words on a picture card or Smartboard. Pictures could tie into curriculum or season of the year (Flags, Sunflowers, Hearts). Have students arrange 16 motion cards in a 4 × 4 grid that can be seen by all.
   - Practice doing each motion with the class.
   - Play the music you have selected while students perform each motion 8 × before moving to the next motion.
   - Teacher cues when to begin.

COMMON MOVEMENTS			
• King Tut	• Hitch Hike	• Scissors	• Flap Wings
• Jump	• Shrug shoulders	• Windshield Wipers	• Twist
• March	• Pat	• Clap hands	• Knock Knees
• Snap	• Click tongue	• Lasso	• Tap shoulders
• Arm roll	• Chicken wings	• Click heels	• Head nod

EXPERIENCES WITH PULSE AND RHYTHM

1. Using rhythm sticks have students echo the teacher's 4-beat patterns.
2. Standing in a circle, take turns creating and echoing 4-beat patterns with rhythm sticks, beginning with the teacher and moving around the circle.
   - Have a student or teacher keep a steady beat on a drum.
   - Challenge: Go completely around the circle without breaking the steady beat.
3. Students demonstrate both rhythm and steady beat concepts by alternately clapping beat versus rhythm, while a well-known song like "Jingle Bells" is being played.
   - Teacher calls out "Beat" or "Rhythm."
   - Make a visual sign where one side says "Beat" and the other side says "Rhythm." Teacher flips sign to indicate when to change.

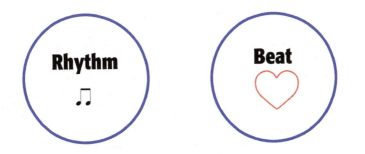

4. Keeping a steady beat, sit/stand in a circle and play the game, "Who Stole the Cookie from the Cookie Jar?"

Teacher:	Who stole the cookie from the cookie jar?
Teacher:	[Name of student] stole the cookie from the cookie jar.
Student:	Who me?
ALL:	Yes, you!
Student:	Couldn't be!
ALL:	Then who?
Student:	[name of another student] stole the cookie from the cookie jar. (continue rhyme)

Challenge: Play the game until every student is named without breaking the beat.

5. ZAP Math Rhythm game (also known as BUZZ). This is a cross-curricular activity using music steady beat and Math.

- Line up students in a line or circle.
- Pick a number (1–12), for example: 4. As the teacher beats a slow rhythm with sticks on a drum, the students begin counting one at a time, when a multiple of 4 is next the student says ZAP instead. If a multiple is missed (or the beat is missed), the student sits down and you start over counting from one. Teacher restarts the beat and gives the cue when to start.
- The person left standing is the winner!
- Try the game again with a different number or a faster steady beat.

Extension: This game can be used with all multiples (multiplication and division fact families).

EXPERIENCES WITH READING AND WRITING NOTATION

1. Rhythm with State Names

Students will understand and use simple music notation, progressing from experience to word/picture symbols to standard notation (quarter note, two eighth notes, four sixteenth notes, one eighth note, and two sixteenth notes combinations, half note, dotted half note, whole note, and the quarter, half, and whole rests).

Teacher makes a set of cards with a picture of a state, labeled with its name on one side. The other side shows the notation and the name of the note. Make enough sets for every two students to share.

♩	Quarter	Maine
♫	2 Eighths	Texas, Kansas, Utah
♬♬	4 Sixteenths	Mississippi, Alabama, Arizona, Colorado, Massachusetts, Minnesota
♪♬	1 Eighth + 2 Sixteenths	Rhode Island
♬♪	2 Sixteenths + 1 Eighth	Delaware, Idaho, Iowa, Tennessee
♩♩♩³	Triplet or triola	Washington
♩	Half note	State (draw this word out over 2 beats)
♩.	Dotted half note	State (draw this word out over 3 beats)
o	Whole note	State (draw this word out over 4 beats)

- Have students turn all the cards picture side up and read them, saying each card on one beat. "Maine, Texas, Mississippi, Rhode Island, Delaware, State (two beats), quarter rest.
- Two students work collaboratively with one set of cards to create two lines of rhythm (four beats each). Take turns sharing the rhythm sentences with the class.
- Combine two teams and have the four students create another 8-beat pattern from their cards and read aloud to the class.
- Turn over the cards and show notation.
2. Explain duration chart:

DURATION	SOUND	SYMBOL	DURATION SYLLABLES
One beat	One sound	♩ Quarter note	Maine
One beat	Silent pulse	𝄽 Quarter rest	(Maine)
One beat	Two sounds	♫ Two Eighth notes	Texas
One beat	Four sounds	♬♬ Four Sixteenth notes	Alabama
One beat	Three sounds	♪♬ One eighth plus Two sixteenths	Rhode Island

		Two sixteenths plus One eighth	
One beat	Three sounds	Idaho	
One beat	Three even sounds	Triplet or Triola	Washington
Two beats	One sound	Half note	Sta—ate
Two beats	Two silent pulses	Half note rest	(Sta—ate)
Three beats	One sound	Dotted half note	Sta—a—ate
Four beats	One sound	Whole note	Sta—a—a—ate
Four beats	Four silent pulses	Whole note rest	(Sta—a—a—ate)

3. Speech Pieces
   Pat the steady beat as you speak the rhymes. Listen for how many sounds you hear on each beat.

   - "Fudge, Fudge" speech piece. Example using quarter notes and eighth notes:

   4/4   Fudge,   fudge   call the   judge

   Ma—ma's   got a   ba -   by

   Not a   girl   not a   boy

   just a   plain 'ole ba -   by.

   - "Apples, Peaches"

   4/4   Ap—ples   peach—es   pears and   plums

   Tell me   when your   birth—day   comes!

Apple, Peaches Birthday Game directions:

   - Game Formation: circle, standing. Keep a steady beat (their choice—shoulders, lap, hands, etc.) while reciting speech piece on the "A" section (apples, peaches, etc.).

   - On the "B" section "January, step in, February step in, March step in . . . ." (months of the year) students with that birthday month step inside the circle and continue reciting the rest of the "B" section.

   - End with "Apples, peaches, pears and plums, now your birthday time has come."

- Melody: This speech piece can be sung on sol-mi-la.

- Extension: The months of the year can be said in Spanish or another language common to the children.

Application

Write practice examples of 4-beat rhythms using notation.

-
-
-

Draw bar lines and double bar lines to show measures in a rhythm sentence.

-
-
-

Read and tap with rhythm sticks 4-beat and 8-beat rhythm examples.

-
-

Underline the beats:

- Bee, Bee Bumblebee"

$\frac{4}{4}$ Bee,   bee   bum-ble   bee.

Stung a   man   on his   knee.

Stung a   pig   on his   snout.

I de-   clare that   you are   out.

- "Cobbler, Cobbler"

$\frac{4}{4}$ Cob-bler,   cob-bler   mend my   shoe.

Get it   done by   half past   two.

Half past   two is   much too   late.

Get it   done by   half past   eight.

Notate these rhymes:

- "Coca Cola"

$\frac{4}{4}$ _____   _____   _____   _____

Co-ca   Co-la   went to   town

_____   _____   _____   _____

Di-et   Pepsi   knocked him   down.

_____   _____   _____   _____

Doc-tor   Pep-per   fixed him   up,

_____   _____   _____   _____

Now we   all drink   Se-ven   Up.

- "Good, Better, Best"

$\frac{4}{4}$ _____   _____   _____   _____

Good,   bet-ter   best,

_____   _____   _____   _____

Nev-er   let it   rest,

| —— | —— | —— | —— |
| 'Til your | good is | bet-ter | and your |

| —— | —— | —— | —— |
| Bet-ter | is | best! | |

- "Red, White and Blue"

$\frac{4}{4}$

| —— | —— | —— | —— |
| Red, | white and | blue, | |

| —— | —— | —— | —— |
| Stars and | stripes for | you. | |

| —— | —— | —— | —— |
| Stars and | stripes for | U S | A, |

| —— | —— | —— | —— |
| Red, | white and | blue. | |

- "Chicken on the Fence Post"

$\frac{4}{4}$

| —— | —— | —— | —— |
| Chick-en on the | fence post | can't dance | Jo-sie, |

| —— | —— | —— | —— |
| Chick-en on the | fence post | can't dance | Jo-sie, |

| —— | —— | —— | —— |
| Chick-en on the | fence post | can't dance | Jo-sie, |

| —— | —— | —— | —— |
| Hel-lo | Su-san | Brown-ie | o! |

Challenge:—Rewrite this poem. Underline the beats and notate the rhythm:

- "Thunder, Lightning"

4/4   Thunder, lightning, rain, rain,

Water down the drain, drain.

Sunshine puts it back again,

Thunder lightning, rain, rain.

1. Rhythm Assessment:

Have students practice writing rhythm notation using **Time Signatures** (2/4, 3/4, and 4/4), **bar lines, measures,** and **double bar lines.**

Use each time signature and write a 4 measure lines of rhythm.

- 2/4

- 3/4

- 4/4

Write the correct rhythm notation dictated by the teacher using 4 measures of rhythm in 4/4 time.

- 4/4

- 4/4

What else can we do with rhythm? Create a content chant to reinforce information you want to remember. Chants can integrate with other subject areas to highlight key points, introduce vocabulary or a concept to reinforce what you have been studying. A silly chant can be used as a "brain break" to help re-focus student attention in a fun way.

TIP BOX

- A time/meter signature is the notation used to specify how many beats are in a measure, and which note value is equivalent to a beat.
- Bar lines are vertical lines that separate the divisions of the time/meter signature.
- A measure is the space between two bar lines.
- Double bar lines are used to separate sections of music or to end a musical piece.

CREATIVE CLASS CHANT ASSIGNMENT

- Chant #1: Use the following poem as a foundation for whatever subject you are studying. Choose three to four vocabulary words from your subject and have your class divide into four groups. Example: Artic Animals.

Group 1: Recites poem

Let's ex-amine this to-day,
So that we know what to say.
Our ob-jec-tive in this class,
Is to learn it really fast.

Take four words and keep the beat
Put it in your hands and feet.
Our ob-jec-tive in this class,
Is to learn and make it last!

Group 2:

Polar Bear

Group 3:

Artic fox

Group 4:

Orca, orca, orca, orca

Speak the poem, layer in your vocabulary words.
Extension: Add instruments to the repeated words.

- Chant #2: Make a group of three to four students. Collaborate and discuss choosing an elementary curriculum subject other than music. Create a rhythmic, content chant that will be performed for the class. Start by gathering important, factual information that an elementary student has to remember. Arrange this information in a four line rhyme, four beats to a line. Notate the rhythm, keeping it simple. Do not sing or use a song for this assignment. It must be an original, creative idea. Once the rhyme is complete, decide how your group will perform it for the class. You may add ostinati, body percussion, or instruments to enhance your performance.

Examples:

Red, blue, indigo, green
Colors, colors, that I've seen
Pink, yellow, orange, white
Which one will you pick tonight?

Say the white piano keys
A, B, C, D, E, F, G
Say them backwards every day
G, F, E, D, C, B, A

Brush, brush, brush your teeth
Every morning, every night
Floss, Floss, Floss your teeth
Keep them shining, pearly white!

INTEGRATION OF MUSIC WITH ELA

PICTURE BOOK ASSIGNMENT

Choose a child's picture book that has strong internal rhythm or a repeated, rhythmic phrase. Using that phrase or creating a NEW phrase, plan when and where the class will say the phrase as you read the story. Instruments, visuals, or hand motions can be added. Write a lesson and plan using this format:

PICTURE BOOK TEMPLATE

Integration of Music with ELA
Grade Level:
Book Title:
Author:
ISBN #:
Music Objective:
Specific Objective:
Materials: (if needed)
Repeated Rhythmic Phrase:
Process:
"Attention Grabber"
Discussion and learning the rhythmic phrase
Read the story
Extensions:
Reflection: To be completed and turned in after you have read the story to the class, describe three things that went well and three things you would do differently.

See Book List Suggestions, Appendix C.

PICTURE BOOK LESSON EXAMPLES

1. Integration of Music with ELA
Grade Level: K, 1
Book Title: "Possum Come A-Knockin'"
Author: Nancy Van Laan, Illustrator: George Booth
Publisher and ISBN #: Dragonfly Books, ISNB 0-679-83468-0, #13: 9780679834687
Music Objective: Through creative expression, students apply their music literacy and the critical-thinking skills of music to sing, play, read, write, and/or move.
Specific Objective: TSW will feel the cadence of the southern dialect and fill in the missing two beats with "Knocking" sounds at the end of the repeated phrase.

Repeated Rhythmic Phrase: "Possum come a knockin' at the door."

Process:

- Can you make a sound with your mouth or hands that sounds like someone is knocking at the door? (Let children explore sounds.)
- When you heard a knock, did you ever open the door to find no one is there? (Get answers.)
- Tell the students that this is a story about a Possum who plays a trick on a little boy who lives in a cabin in the mountains.
- Ask your students to listen to you read the first two lines of the book and ask for them to naturally add the knocking sounds they think are missing. (They should answer with two strong beats.).
- Read the two lines and have children respond. Tell them to add those two strong knocks every time you read that phrase during the story.
- Read the book with dramatic and fun expression.
- Ask students if there were any action words that they did not understand. Explain (whittling, etc.).

Extensions: Read the story again, but instead of making the knocking sounds with body percussion, hand out rhythm instruments that could sound like knocking. (Wood blocks, rhythm sticks, etc.).

Reflection:

2. Integration of Music with ELA
Grade Level: K, 1
Book Title: "Trashy Town"
Author: Andrea Zimmerman and David Clemesha.
Publisher and ISBN #: Harper Collins Publishers, ISBN 0-06-027139-6.
Grade Level: K, 1
Music Objective: Through *creative expression*, students apply their music literacy and the critical-thinking skills of music to sing, play, read, write, and/or *move*.
Specific Objective: TSW listen to and find the pattern in the story Trashy Town. TSW learn a hand.jive pattern to perform each time the rhythmic pattern is repeated.

Process:

- How many of you have seen or heard the trash truck driving down your street? (Wait for answers)
- Where else do you think the trash truck has been, or where is he going? (Wait for answers)
- Let's read a story about the trashman Mr. Gilly and see all the places he goes to collect the trash.
- Begin the story. When you read the first rhythmic phrase, pause and ask your students to help you with the phrase.
- Add the hand jive motions.

Repeated Rhythmic Phrase:

<u>Dump it in</u>, <u>smash it down</u>, <u>drive a</u>—<u>round the</u> <u>trashy town</u>.

> Students pound one fist into the other two times while saying "Dump it in";
> Add "<u>clap, clap, clap</u>."
> Students pat legs two times while saying, "<u>Smash it down</u>,"
> Add "<u>clap, clap, clap</u>."
> Students pretend to steer a truck while saying, "<u>Drive a</u>—<u>round the</u> <u>trash-y town</u>."

Continue and finish the story, encouraging students to participate with the repeated phrase.

Extensions: Teacher encourages children to vocalize expressive words during the story, that is, "No," "Stop," and "Up, up, up and Down, down, down." (Teacher is able to give nonverbal cues, i.e., moving hands up/down.)

Reflection:

3. Integration of Music with ELA
Grade Level: 3
Book Title: Totally Tardy Marty
Author: Erica S. Perl, Illustrator: Jarrett J. Krosoczka   ISBN #: 9781419716614
Music Objective: Through creative expression, students apply their music literacy and the critical-thinking skills of music **to *sing, play,*** read, write, and/or move.
Specific Objective: TSW identify repeated phrases in the story Totally Tardy Marty. Create a *melody (using tones that we know) and to play a game.*

Process:
"Have you ever been late to something important?" "What was it?"

- Ask students to listen for what happens in the story, what makes Marty late. Is there a place in the story for a tune?
- **Read the story.**
- **Ask students for answers to your questions (what happens in the story or what happens to the main character). (Write your answer here).**

Extension: On second reading of story guide students in creating a short song to sing "Totally Tardy Marty"; Never Late Kate/Nate; Great.

Reflection:

4. Integration of Music with ELA
Grade Level: 3rd and 4th
Book Title: Rap a Tap Tap Here's Bojangles-Think of that! **Author:** Leo & Diane Dillon
Publisher and ISBN #: Scholastic, ISBN 0-439-56066-7
Music Objective: Through **creative expression**, students apply their music literacy and the critical-thinking skills of music to sing, **play**, read, write, and/or **move**.

Specific Objective: TSW identify the recurring speech pattern. TSW put the rhythm of the text in their feet.

Repeated Rhythmic Phrase: Rap a tap tap, here's Bojangles, think of that!

Process:

- Attention Grabber—Have you ever taken a dance class or dance lessons?
- Ask students: Listen for what happens in the story. Do you hear any sentences that are repeated?
- Read the story.
- Ask students for answers to your questions (what happens in the story or what happens to the main character). (Write your answer here).

Extensions:

- Have students identify the repeated sentence and first play it on their hands.
- After two pages the S. transfers the pattern from hands to lap.
- After another two pages the S., transfer the pattern to feet standing up. Half of the sentence in one foot—the other half in the other foot.
- After another two pages, S. will add individual style (such as arm motions and turns).

Reflection:

PICTURE BOOK ASSIGNMENT RUBRIC

I. Rhythmic Chant				
• Direct pattern from book	0	1		
• Addition of body percussion, Movement, or instruments	0	1	2	3
II Presentation and Written Directions				
• Clear explanation to class, Effectiveness engaging students	0	1	2	3
• Speaking Skills—volume, easily understood, expression Book facing class, eye contact	0	1	2	3
• Format of lesson plan	0	1		
• Information on the book: Title, Author, Publisher, ISBN#	0	1		
• Easy to follow written directions	0	1	2	
• Extensions	0	1		

/15

More Lesson Examples for Your Classroom using Rhythm and Cross-Curricular Subjects

ENGLISH LANGUAGE ARTS—ELA

1. Additional Speech Pieces

- *O-C-T-O-B-E-R*

  O-C-T-O-B-E-R
  Halloween brings a candy bar.
  On the 12th is a holiday.
  Fall is here and winter's on it's way. Brr! I like October.

- *One, Two, Tie My Shoe:*

  One, two, tie my shoe. Three, four, shut the door.
  Five, six, pick up sticks. Seven, eight, lay them straight.
  Nine, ten, a big fat hen.

- Fill in the blank speech pieces:

  What did you do over Spring Break? "I <u>went to the zoo</u>."
  Keeping a steady beat, continue around the circle letting each child fill in the blank.

Songs—Experiencing rhyming words in a song,

- "A-Hunting We Will Go"

  Pat and clap the beat only during refrain.
  Extension: What other animals could you use to make your own rhyming words?

- Echo songs with rhyming words, "Down By the Bay."

SCIENCE

- Help your students create a chant using vocabulary words and facts they have been working with in your classroom, such as plants, water cycle, clouds, insects, birds, flowers, ...

SOCIAL STUDIES

- Citizenship—Use nonlocomotor movements to keep a steady beat while listening to the National March, "Stars and Stripes Forever."
- Have an instrument play along with specific rhythms assigned to the sections or form of the music.

MATH

- Create new chants using Nursery rhymes as math word problems. Examples:

Original:
Hush Little Baby, Don't say a word,
Papa's gonna buy you a mockingbird.
If that Mockingbird don't sing,
Papa's gonna buy you a diamond ring.

Math version:
Hush Little Baby Don't say a word
Mama's going to buy you 5 mockingbirds
and if I take away 3 mockingbirds
Mama's going to be left with how many birds? _____

Original:
Rub a Dub Dub, three men in a tub,
and who do you think they see?
A butcher, a baker, a candlestick maker,
they all sailed out to sea.

Math version:
Rub a Dub Dub, three men in a tub, but
six more jumped right in. More
butchers and bakers but the candlestick maker
jumped out and said, "I'll swim!"

How many men were left in the tub? _____

- Upper Elementary game song, "Weevily Wheat" multiplication tables sung in a movement game.

Chapter Reflection: List below the music activity and/or song used in this chapter to connect MUSIC with another elementary subject.

MUSIC ACTIVITY AND/OR SONG:	OBJECTIVE: GRADE LEVEL
ELA	
Science	
Social Studies	
Math	
Health/PE	
Theatre/Art	

ENGAGING CHILDREN WITH MELODY

CHAPTER 3

Chapter Objectives

After completing this chapter, you will be able to:

- Know the difference between pitch and melody.
- Read music notation for pitch.
- Describe melody using standard music vocabulary: step, skip, leap, interval, phrase, and melodic contour.
- Play the recorder using B A G pitches.

Vocabulary

Pitch—The quality of sound governed by the rate of vibrations producing the highness and lowness of a tone.

Melody—A musical sentence of pitches that can move up, down, have steps, have skips, and can have repeating notes, which creates a "tune" or song when combined with rhythm.

Interval—The distance between two pitches.

Melodic Contour—The direction of the melody, which can be seen on the staff or heard as you sing.

Skill Development

EXPERIENCING PITCH: HIGH AND LOW

These activities will help children increase their awareness of sounds, identify the source and describe what they hear.

- Recognize environmental sounds. Sit quietly, close your eyes and make a list of the sounds you hear.
- Name sounds from these categories: animals, machines, and nature. Pictures would provide helpful cues.
- Instruments—Listen for High and Low pitches in music examples. Music Suggestions: "Peter and the Wolf" by Prokofiev, "Chinese Dance" from the Nutcracker by Tchaikovsky, "Aquarium" by Saint-Saens.
- Melodic Contour—Sing Song examples with wavy line showing direction of melody: up, down, stays the same (suggestions: Row, Row your Boat; Bow Wow Wow; Merrily We Roll Along). Discuss the concept of a musical phrase/sentence and show examples in the songs.

EXPERIENCING TRANSITION FROM CONTOUR TO STANDARD NOTATION

- Learn the song "Apple Tree" (Music Library) and play its game.
- Let's look at what the pitches of this song might look like if we had a picture of how high, how low, or whether the pitch stayed the same. Take a piece of paper and place it on top of the apples. Trace a line from one note to the next. This is called the melodic contour and shows the direction your voice should go.

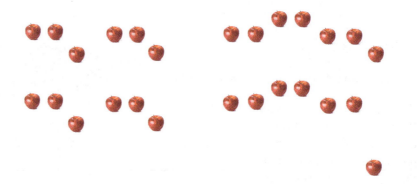

- Next, put the apples on the music staff. Sing the song again and follow the apples.

Apple tree, apple tree

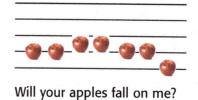

Will your apples fall on me?

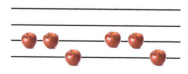

I won't cry, I won't shout,

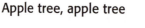

If your apples knock me out!

- Compare the skips, steps, and leaps.
- Find the lowest pitch.

● Compare the apples to the notes on the staff:

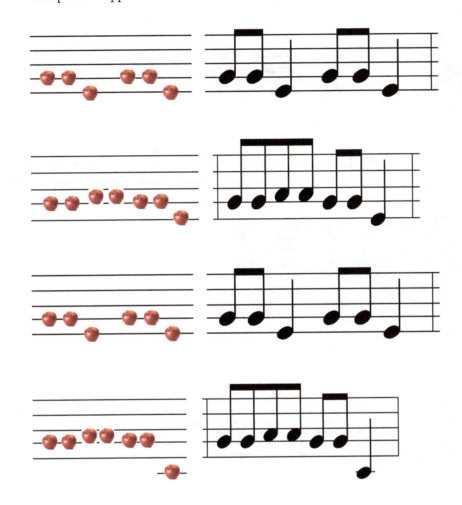

EXPERIENCING STANDARD NOTATION

● Label all the notes for the treble clef (line notes, space notes, placement on grand staff, treble staff, and music alphabet).

Staff:

Treble Clef:

Bass Clef:

Lines—how many lines? (5) Starting from the bottom, say the sentence "Every Good Boy Does Fine".

E G B D F

Spaces—How many spaces? (4, between the 5 lines) Remember, "Space" rhymes with "F A C E"

F A C E

Put them both together—what pattern do you see?

Treble Clef notes

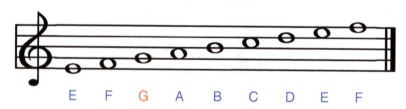

E F G A B C D E F

Grand Staff notes

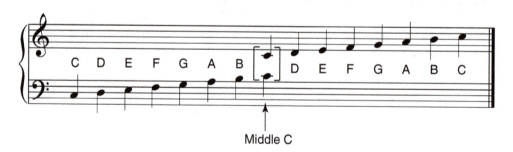

C D E F G A B   D E F G A B C

Middle C

1. Play a musical flash card game, "Around the World" by showing a card to two students. The student that first speaks the note name correctly moves to the next student to try again on a new note.

2. Practice Naming Pitches on Staff

   • Fill in the staff with notes to spell the words in the story.

"A HEN NAMED DEB"

© GraphicsRF/Shutterstock.com

Once there was a pretty little farm on a pretty little hill on the (edge) _____ of

a pretty little forest. Farmer (Ed) _____ had many animals on his pretty little

farm. His favorite was a pretty little hen named, (Deb) _____. She gave Farmer

(Ed) _____ a pretty little white (egg) _____ to eat every morning for breakfast

so he would not have to drive to a (cafe) _____ in town. One morning,

(Deb) _____ saw a pretty little Robin bird, who flew down to (gab) _____

with (Deb) _____. "Fiddle (dee,dee)! _____ How do you (Be)"?, _____ said

the Robin. "Not (bad)" _____ said "Deb" _____ "Look at my pretty little Blue

TIP BOX

• Those students who have previously studied music should have a limit of how far they can move at a time.

• Free treble clef cards can be found on the Internet.

(egg)" ▬▬▬, said the Robin, pointing to her nest in the nearby tree. Then a pretty

little Warbler bird flew down and said," Look at my pretty little red (egg) ▬▬▬!"

Then a pretty little Thrush bird flew down and (gabbed) ▬▬▬, "Look at my

Spotted (egg) ▬▬▬!" "Wow" said "(Deb) ▬▬▬ and wished her plain, little

white (egg) ▬▬▬ could be a beautiful color too! "Should I (dab) ▬▬▬ some

paint on my (egg) ▬▬▬?" she wondered. "Or (add) ▬▬▬ colored paper to

my (egg) ▬▬▬? Maybe I just need to eat a special (feed) ▬▬▬ with color!"

At dinner time, she (begged) ▬▬▬ Farmer (Ed) for something new to eat. Being a

little (deaf) ▬▬▬ he didn't quite understand. Farmer (Ed) ▬▬▬ gave her some

pretty little (cabbage) ▬▬▬ that grew next to the hen house. But her (egg) ▬▬▬

did not turn green. The next day, he (fed) ▬▬▬ her some pretty little carrots.

But her (egg) ▬▬▬ did not turn orange. He tried a (feedbag) ▬▬▬ of beets, but

her (egg) ▬▬▬ did not turn purple. Farmer (Ed) ▬▬▬ thought and thought.

Then, (Abe) ▬▬▬ the (Bee) ▬▬▬ flew over and buzzed a new idea into his

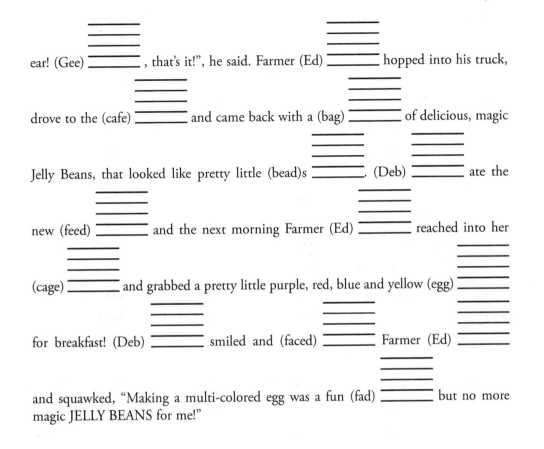

ear! (Gee) ———— , that's it!", he said. Farmer (Ed) ———— hopped into his truck,

drove to the (cafe) ———— and came back with a (bag) ———— of delicious, magic

Jelly Beans, that looked like pretty little (bead)s ————. (Deb) ———— ate the

new (feed) ———— and the next morning Farmer (Ed) ———— reached into her

(cage) ———— and grabbed a pretty little purple, red, blue and yellow (egg) ————

for breakfast! (Deb) ———— smiled and (faced) ———— Farmer (Ed) ————

and squawked, "Making a multi-colored egg was a fun (fad) ———— but no more magic JELLY BEANS for me!"

- Create a story using the words that can be made using the music alphabet (A-G). Each time a word is used, notate the pitches on a treble staff so the word can be decoded on a blank line beside the notes.

Words that can be spelled using the Music Alphabet:

Music	Alphabet	Words		
1 letter	A			
2 letters	Ad	Ed	Fa	
3 letters	Abe	Ace	Add	Age
	Baa	Bad	Bag	Bed
	Bee	Beg		
	Cab	Cad		
	Dab	Dad	Dee	
	Ebb	Egg		
	Fad	Fed		
	Gab	Gag	GED	Gee
4 letters	Abba	Abed	Aced	Aged
	Baba	Babe	Bade	Bead
	Beef			
	Cade	Cafe	Cage	Cede
	Dead	Deaf	Deed	
	Edge	Egad		
	Face	Fade	Feed	
	Gabe	Gaff	Gaga	Gage
5 letters	Adage	Added		
	Badge			
	Caged	Ceded		
	Decaf			
	Ebbed	Edged	Egged	
	Faced	Faded		
	Gaged			
6 letters	Accede			
	Badged	Bagged	Beaded	Beefed
	Begged			
	Dabbed	Decade	Deeded	Deface
	Efface			

	Facade			
	Gabbed	Gaffed	Gagged	
7 letters	Acceded			
	Baggage			
	Cabbage			
	Feedbag			

FURTHER EXPERIENCES WITH MELODY

1. Use Appendix A Music Library to practice reading rhythms and singing melodies of common songs for children.
2. Turn to Chapter 9 Engaging the Recorder and learn songs using the pitches B, A, and G.

MUSIC ACTIVITY AND/OR SONG:	OBJECTIVE: GRADE LEVEL
ELA	
Science	
Social Studies	
Math	
Health/PE	
Theatre/Art	

ENGAGING CHILDREN WITH SINGING

Providing children with a variety of experiences, such as singing, moving, dancing, storytelling, pretending, playing instruments, and listening to music, is integral to the elementary curriculum. This chapter and the following chapters (Chapters 5–8) address these topics.

Singing is a common expression of making music. It can describe cultural traditions, document current and historical events, and tell stories. Through music we can express our own emotions in addition to ones that unite us with various feelings such as love, patriotism, and protest. Common goals and bonds can be strengthened through the power of music.

Chapter Objectives

After completing this chapter, you will be able to:

- Demonstrate various pitch "voices" (speaking, whispering, shouting, singing).
- Use your singing voice tunefully with good vocal techniques.
- Know how to choose an appropriate song for elementary children.
- Integrate songs with cross-curricular lessons.

Vocabulary

Tune—A short piece of music without words, the melody only.

Song—A piece of music with words. It combines melody and vocal singing. The words to a song are called lyrics.

Texture—How rhythm, melody and harmony combine to create layers in the music. A thin texture contains fewer instruments/voices, whereas a thicker texture would have more instruments/voices.

Harmony—The combination of multiple musical pitches sounding simultaneously.

Round—A song that can be sung by two or more groups of people. One group starts the song and the next group starts the same song from the beginning at a designated point. When the first group gets to the end of the song they start again, as does the second and third group. They can go "round and round" singing it several times. This creates harmony.

Partner Songs—Two or more songs with the same meter and chord structure that are sung simultaneously. This creates harmony.

Choir or Chorus—A chorus is a group of singers following a director.
Adult Voices—Adults have more mature vocal muscles and are able to sing a wider range of pitches. Individual voices are labeled Soprano (higher female voice), Alto (lower female voice), Tenor (higher male voice), and Bass (Lower male voice).

Skill Development

CHARACTERISTCS OF CHILDREN'S VOICES

1. There are four voices we use: Speaking, Shouting, Whispering, and Singing. Children need practice and reinforcement to develop these individual ways to use their voices.

   - Choose various short poems and have children use their speaking, shouting, whispering, and singing voices.

© SpeedKingz/Shutterstock.com

VOCAL EXPLORATION

2. Vocal Exploration
   - The book, "How To Speak Moo!" by Deborah Fajerman is an excellent source for the class to read together that explores many ways to say, "Moo."
   - Practice speaking aloud using a "High squeaky voice" like a mouse; a "deep, low" giant or dad's voice, a "shaky" voice like someone is cold or afraid.

CREATIVE DRAMA WITH VOICE EXPLORATION

3. Creative drama with voice exploration
   - Goldilocks and the Three Bears http://www.dltk-teach.com/rhymes/goldilocks_story.htm http://www.dltk-teach.com/rhymes/goldilocks_story.htm
   - The Three Little Pigs http://storyberries.com/the-three-little-pigs/
   - Mr. Wiggle and Mr. Waggle https://guybrarian.files.wordpress.com/2011/11/mr-wiggle-and-mr-waggle.pdf

"PIGGYBACK" SONGS

4. Make use of "Piggyback" songs, or tunes you already know where the words are changed to apply to your classroom.

      •   Tune: "The Ants Go Marching"

We all go marching one by one hurrah, hurrah,
We all go marching one by one hurrah, hurrah,
We all go marching one by one, if you are wearing (green) sit down,
and we'll all keep marching round and round the room boom, boom, boom.
(Repeat using different colors or items of clothing until everyone is seated.)

      •   Tune: "The Addams Family" by Vic Mizzy
          (The X can be a clap, pat or a snap)

Days of the week, X X. Days of the week, X X.
Days of the week, days of the week, days of the week XX.
There's Sunday and there's Monday, there's Tuesday and there's Wednesday,
there's Thursday and there's Friday, and then there's Saturday.
(Repeat the first section of the song.)

GOOD SINGING TECHNIQUES

1. It is important to practice good posture, breathing techniques, and clear diction to set the foundation for lifelong singers. Frequently, remind students to:

    Sit tall
    Stand tall
    Shoulders down
    Relax your jaw
    Breathe deeply
    Support your tone
    Target the pitch
    Sing with clear diction

SINGING SKILL PROGRESSION

2. Singing Skill Progression

Children usually develop singing in the following sequence, from easier to more difficult.

      •   Singing a song in unison—"Long-Legged Sailor" and "The Old Gray Cat"
      •   Echo songs—"Hello There!" and "My Aunt Came Back"
      •   Call and response songs—"John, the Rabbit," "Way Down Yonder in the Brickyard"

TIP BOX

Telling children to sing louder can be harmful to their vocal muscles.

Emphasize proper breathing and breath support and never ask them to yell or shout-sing.

Encourage them to listen to others singing around them so their voice will blend with the choir.

- Rounds (which create simple harmonies)—"Row, Row, Row Your Boat," "Are You Sleeping?"
- Partner songs (which create simple harmonies). Sing at the same time— "Winter Fantasy" which includes the song "Jingle Bells;" "Bow, Wow, Wow" sung with "Hot Cross Buns" or "This Old Man" sung with "Here We Go 'Round the Mulberry Bush".

SINGING ADDS TEXTURE AND HARMONY

TIP BOX

An accompaniment is a musical part that supports a solo instrument, voice, or group.

3. Singing adds Texture and Harmony

Monophonic—A single, unaccompanied melody.

- Sing "Rain, Rain Go Away" to demonstrate monophonic texture.

Homophonic—An accompanied melodic line as in playing chords with Boomwhackers or guitars while you sing.

- Sing "Rain, Rain Go Away" while teacher adds a simple accompaniment on the guitar or piano.

Polyphonic—Two or more independent melodic lines sounding simultaneously resulting in harmony. The melodies can be the same as in a round, or different as in partner songs and descants.

- Sing the round, "A Ram, Sam, Sam" to demonstrate polyphonic texture, resulting in harmony.
- Sing the songs, "Skip to My Lou," "This Old Man," and "Mulberry Bush" separately to demonstrate monophonic texture. Then sing them all together to demonstrate polyphonic texture resulting in harmony.
- Sing "This Train," "When the Saints Go Marching In," and "Swing Low, Sweet Chariot" separately and then all together to demonstrate monophonic and polyphonic texture.

Application
Questions to Answer

1. Singing "Row, Row, Row Your Boat" in a round is an example of _____ _____ texture.
2. A cowboy singing a song while strumming chords on a guitar is an example of _____ texture.
3. A child whistling a tune is an example of _____ texture.
4. When we sing partner songs _____ occurs.

HOW TO CHOOSE AN APPROPRIATE SONG FOR CHILDREN

1.   Children have limited vocal ranges. The **range** of a song is the distance between the lowest and highest pitches in a song.

Lower elementary children can sing songs on the Treble staff from the D below the treble staff to third line B. Upper elementary children have larger vocal muscles and are able to extend their range, usually from Low A to High E. When you choose a song make sure the children are physically able to sing it. Check the range of pitches.

Lower elementary

Upper elementary

2.   Remember what the purpose of the song will be. Is it to be sung in a program about George Washington? Is it to demonstrate singing in a round? Is it to have fun singing common holiday songs? The song chosen should be the best example to match your objective of what the children are learning. Be sensitive to the cultures represented in your school. Be sensitive to the lyrics in the song, making sure each word is appropriate for that age child. Choosing a specific song you think is fine but is connected to an artist parents would object to is probably not the one to choose.

INTEGRATING MULTICULTURAL MUSIC

Thank you Julissa Chapa for sharing these multicultural ideas.
Using music from many cultures has several benefits. It can:

- Raise awareness about the world around us
- Instill respect for the cultures represented within our own country
- Highlight the fact that music is a worldwide phenomenon
- Integrate with social studies curriculum

GENERAL DESCRIPTIONS AND COMMON TRAITS IN WORLD MUSIC

Music of Africa

Although Africa consists of various cultures, ethnic groups and languages, there are similarities in music throughout the continent. These similarities are:

- Music is participatory and communal.
- Pulsating beat is present, as well as driving rhythms.

© Simon Kovacic/Shutterstock.com

- Two or more rhythms are played simultaneously (called polyrhythms) often with contrasting underlying meters.
- Folk instruments include the shekere, djembe, talking drum, and mbira.

Asia
China and Japan

- Music is made up of mostly pentatonic scales.
- Focus is on a melodic line, or variations of the melodic line.
- Tone colors are often interwoven with stringed, percussion, and wind instrument.
- Nature is a common theme, as can be exemplified by the Japanese folk song, Sakura.
- Folk instruments include the erhu, xiao, and koto.

India

- Most Americans became aware of Indian music when George Harrison played the sitar on one of the Beatle albums after studying with Ravi Shankar.
- Folk instruments include the sitar and tabla drums.

Music of Europe

- Folk music from Europe comes from a tradition of ballads telling stories of daily life, heroism and love with beautiful melodies.
- Folk instruments include harps, violins, accordions, recorders. lutes and many more.
- Drones, a persistent tone or tones as a harmonic base in music, such as played by the Scottish bagpipe.

Music from the Americas

- Native American music is unique to the Americas. Common traits are the use of percussion, vocables, and flutes.
- Music from North and South America is derived from European, African and Asian traditions.
- Includes a variety of languages and genres. Example; Latin American music (different in every country), Caribbean music, African-American Spirituals, folk music from Canada, jazz, blues, rock, rap, mariachi, corrido, and Tejano.
- Folk instruments include the Appalachian dulcimer and banjo, original to America.

© Natata/Shutterstock.com

© PRILL/Shutterstock.com

© ZZTop1958/Shutterstock.com

© Kobby Dagan/Shutterstock.com

Sample Songs

- K-2nd grade Kye, Kye, Kule (Africa), Se, Se, Se (Japan), Grinding Corn (Native American), and La Raspa (Mexico)
- 3rd–4th grade Obwisana (Ghana), Sasha (Russia,) Grand Old Duke of York (England), and Four White Horses (Caribbean-Virgin Islands)
- 4th–5rd grade Funga Alafia (Nigeria), I's the B'y (Newfoundland), I Let Her Go-go (Trinidad and Tobago), Aquaqua (Israel), and Follow the Drinking Gourd (African American Spiritual)

From what part of the world is your musical heritage? _____
Can you name a multi-cultural song that is not listed here? _____

Application

- Using song material from Appendix A, Music Library, pick two songs that would be appropriate for grades K-2 and select two songs for grades 3–5. List reasons for your choices.

Grades K–2
Song Title   Why is this song appropriate?

1.

2.

Grades 3–5
Song Title   Why is this song appropriate?

1.

2.

- Why do you think singing activities are important for children to experience?

_____

_____

Chapter Reflection: List below the music activity and/or song used in this chapter to connect MUSIC with another elementary subject.

MUSIC ACTIVITY AND/OR SONG:	OBJECTIVE: GRADE LEVEL
ELA	
Science	
Social Studies	
Math	
Health/PE	
Theatre/Art	

ENGAGING CHILDREN WITH PLAYING MELODIC AND RHYTHMIC INSTRUMENTS

The addition of instruments in making music goes back to the beginning of human history. Log drums, carved flutes and strings vibrating all contributed to the experiences of creating rhythmic and melodic music. Children love to play instruments and playing them together builds not only their music skills but stronger relationships and community. Added bonuses occur when children learn the science behind the acoustics of sound, experience the creative thrill involved with sound stories in ELA, discover world wide cultural instruments and discover ways to reinforce math concepts.

Chapter Objectives

- Identify Pitched and Unpitched instruments.
- Demonstrate chord accompaniment with a simple melody.
- Play a variety of elementary classroom instruments.
- Integrate instruments in cross-curricular lessons.

Vocabulary

Pitched percussion instruments produce a pitch by striking instruments such as the xylophone, piano, choir chimes, glockenspiel, and boomwhackers.

Unpitched percussion instruments produce a unique timbre by striking, shaking or scraping (maracas, finger cymbals, wood blocks, triangles, guiros, etc.)

Timbre is the unique tone color and character of an individual voice or musical sound.

Ostinato is a rhythmic, melodic, or harmonic phrase that repeats over and over under the melody.

Chord is a group of pitches (typically three) played together that combine to create harmony. A pitched percussion instrument can play a chord accompaniment while you sing the melody of a song.

Form is the overall structure or plan of a piece of music, usually organized in sections.

Accompaniment is music that supports a melody line harmonically. For example, the pianist played an accompaniment as the choir sang.

Ensemble is a group of musicians making music together.

Skill Development

EXPERIENCES WITH UNPITCHED PERCUSSION

1. Rhythmic Ostinato

   • Sing "Bounce High, Bounce Low". Clap an ostinato as you sing the song again.

   a. ♩ ♫♩ ♩

   b. ♫♩ ♫♩

Extension: Choose an unpitched percussion instrument to accompany a song of your choice with one of the rhythmic ostinatos.

2. Melodic Ostinato

   • Sing the song, "Yonder Come Day" from Appendix A and extract a phrase to sing along with the song, i.e. "Yonder come day"—repeat or "Oh my soul"—repeat

3. Reading or playing rhythmic patterns while accompanying music

   • Prepare students to play rhythmic instruments to the "Stars and Stripes Forever" by John Philip Sousa

   a. Discuss John Philip Sousa, the composer. Key information includes National March, Sousaphone, and the Marine Corp Band.

   b. Divide into four groups with instruments (See the key naming the triangle, maracas, drums and sticks with their symbol of when to play).

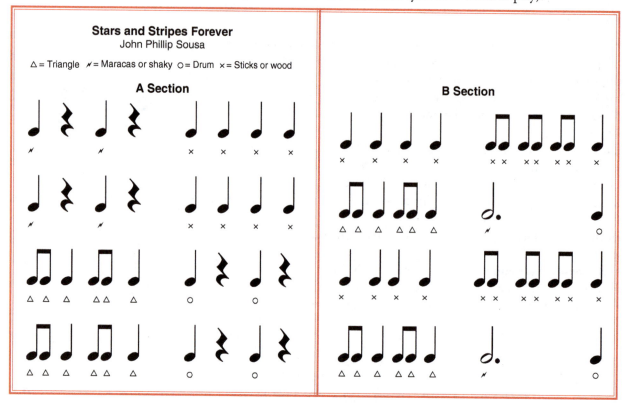

C Section

Hurrah for the flag of the free
May it wave as our standard forever,
The gem of the land and the sea
The banner of the right
Let despots remember the day,
When our fathers with mighty endeavor,
Proclaimed as they marched to the fray,
That by their might and by their right it waves forever.

D Section

c. Practice your rhythm part

d. Practice section C singing lyrics to the tune. Go over any vocabulary children do not understand.

• The form for this song is AABBCDCDC. To give you more playing time, follow this pattern for the instruments AABBCDABDAB.

Thank you to our music teacher friend, Evelyn Smith, for sharing her activity.

4. Percussion instruments are divided into three categories depending upon how their sound is produced. These categories are scraping, shaking, or striking. Some instruments can fit in more than one category.

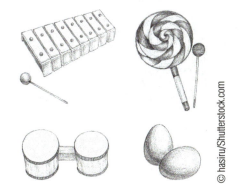

© hasiru/Shutterstock.com

What is the name of this instrument and what sounds will it produce? _____

© Babyboom/Shutterstock.com

5. Create your own percussion instrument.

• Example 1: Fill a plastic egg with rice and use for a shaker. Read the book, "Rattlesnake Dance" by Jim Arnosky and cue children when to shake their egg.

• Example 2: Make rainsticks, look online for simple directions. Read the book, "Bringing the Rain to Kapiti Plain" by Verna Aardema. Cue the children for rain sounds.

• Have children make a variety of instruments. Write out 3 or 4 rhythm lines for them to practice playing. Divide into groups. layer the patterns to build texture and create an ensemble.

EXPERIENCES WITH PITCHED PERCUSSION

Pitched percussions instruments can play the musical alphabet, A B C D E F G.

Playing from A to A, B to B, C to C, etc. with the pattern of whole step, whole step, half step, whole step, whole step, whole step, half step is called a major scale.

These pitches can be labeled Do, Re, Mi, Fa, Sol, La, Ti, Do (Remember "Do-Re-Mi" from the Sound of Music?) or with numbers or Roman numerals.

A major scale in the key of C is played:
C D E F G A B C'

Fill in the chart:

INSTRUMENT NAME	CATEGORY (SCRAPE, SHAKE OR STRIKE)	MELODIC OR RHYTHMIC	WHAT IS IT MADE OF?
Wood Block	Strike	R	wood
Maraca			
Guiro			
Piano			
Triangle			
Glockenspiel			
Tambourine			
Hand Drum			
Sticks			
Boomwhackers			
Xylophone			
Sleigh Bells			
Finger Cymbals			

Experiences With Pitched Percussion

Thank you to Julissa Chapa for sharing these chord progression charts.

You can create simple accompaniments for songs by playing chords. A chord is a group of pitches (typically three) played together that combine to create harmony. On every pitch of a major scale a chord can be built.

Chord Progressions

- Chords are labeled by its placement as well as its letter name.
  These numbers are usually denoted with Roman numerals. Capital numerals indicate a major chord, while lowercase numerals indicate a minor chord.

C	D	E	F	G	A	B	C
1	2	3	4	5	6	7	1
I	ii	iii	IV	V	vi	vii°	I

Chord Progressions

In most Western music, chord progressions start on I and end on I.

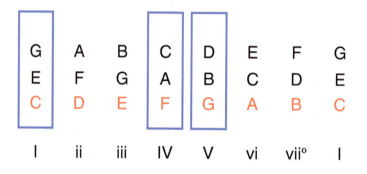

- The most powerful chords of the sequence are I, IV, and V.
- Notice how some chords share pitches.
- Practice this simple chord progression:

Play the I chord for 8 beats
Play the IV chord for 8 beats
Play the V chord for 8 beats
Play the I chord for 8 beats.

- Pick a song from Appendix A, Music Library such as "A Sailor Went to Sea" and notice the C and G chord symbols above the music. To play a simple accompaniment, play on the beat until the chord changes.
- Play this 12 bar (measure) Blues chord progression using the I IV and V chords in the key of C:

```
I    I    I    I
IV   IV   I    I
V    V    I    I
```

APPLICATION

Pitched Percussion Instruments and Recorder Assessments

Directions: READ EVERYTHING BEFORE PLAYING INSTRUMENTS.

1. Make teams of 4 persons.
2. You will have 15–20 minutes each for station.
3. Work quickly so you will be ready for the assessment at the end of each station.
4. Work as a team and do assessments as a team. As much as possible, make sure everyone has an equal part to play.
5. Signal the teacher when your team is ready for assessment.

Station 1 Piano

1. Using your right hand, practice playing "Merrily We Roll Along" on the piano.
2. Play individually for assessment.

Station 2 Boomwhackers

1. Lay out on the floor the Boomwhacker pitches C to C (one octave-Do, Re, Mi, etc.) in order.
2. Discuss: List other instruments that are similar to Boomwhackers and tell why.

_____

_____

_____

3. Discuss: What "sound" science (acoustic) principles can you deduce from how Boomwhackers create sound?

_____

_____

_____

4. Compare/contrast how sounds are made on a recorder versus Boomwhackers.

_____

_____

_____

5. Work as a team to play "Jingle Bells".
6. Play the song for assessment.

Station 3 Glockenspiels/Xylophone

1. Read about Carl Orff, Chapter 1.
2. Review holding the mallet and mallet technique.
3. Play "Juba" for assessment.

Station 4 Choir Chimes (if available)

1. This is a DELICATE instrument! Hold handle only. DO NOT TOUCH the bell mechanism. The chime mechanism should face you while you play. Take off rings, bracelets, necklaces, watches, etc that may scratch the surface of the chime.

2. Move your arm in a forward circular manner, moving down and away from you. Snap your wrist at the upward part of the arc. Continue the circle to bring the chime back in front of you. A hammer motion is incorrect.
3. Play the tune "Flowers" for assessment.

Station 5 Recorder

1. Practice and play for assessment the assigned song this week.

Station 6 Boomwhackers II/Bell Sets

1. Organize the Boomwhackers to play chord accompaniment for "Lil' Liza Jane".
2. Decide how to play chords while you sing the song.
3. Signal when your team is ready to play for assessment.
4. Bonus: Add recorder part and perform.

Why do you think music instrument activities are important for children to experience?

_____

_____

Chapter Reflection: List below the music activity and/or song used in this chapter to connect MUSIC with another elementary subject.

MUSIC ACTIVITY AND/OR SONG:	OBJECTIVE: GRADE LEVEL
ELA	
Science	
Social Studies	
Math	
Health/PE	
Theatre/Art	

ENGAGING CHILDREN WITH LISTENING

What is it that appeals to you in the music you enjoy? Is it a catchy rhythmic pattern? The unique timbre or sound of a voice or instrument? The way multiple singers or instrument players relate to each other? Listening to music helps develop an appreciation of different music styles, cultures and composers. Students can reinforce their knowledge of music elements and integrate their music experience with other subjects. This chapter will enable you to actively listen to and analyze the music you enjoy and how to share this concept with your students.

Chapter Objectives

After completing this chapter, you will be able to:

- Identify vocal timbre.
- Identify symphonic instrument timbre.
- Identify the four families of symphonic and world instruments.
- Identify expressive elements in music.
- Identify form in music.
- Analyze music in reference to the seven elements of music.
- Create a Listening Map.
- Integrate Listening activities with cross-curricular lessons.

Vocabulary

Expressive—Nuances in the music, such as dynamics and tempo, that make the music come alive.

Form—The overall structure or plan of a piece of music, usually organized in sections.

Skill Development

LISTENING AWARENESS

1. Environmental Sounds.

   - In chapter 3, students had an activity listening to environmental sounds regarding the concept of high and low. Review that activity and answer the following questions.

What do you hear in the classroom?
What do you hear outside?
What do you hear when you are at home sitting in your living room?
What do you hear as you are riding in a car?

- Fill in the chart with sounds you hear in each category.

PEOPLE	MACHINE	NATURE	ANIMAL

- Have someone out of sight in the room explore various sounds made by common items such as paper being crumpled or ripped, pencils tapped or scraped against wood or metal.

2. What's in your music library? Play various music selections and describe what you hear in the chart.

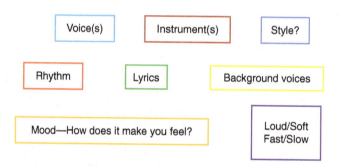

MUSIC SELECTION	VOICE(S) OR INSTRUMENT(S)	STYLE	RHYTHM	LYRICS	MOOD	LOUD/SOFT FAST/SLOW?

VOCAL TIMBRE

- Listen to examples of adult timbre, Soprano, Alto, Tenor, and Bass. Describe the voices in each selection.

George Frideric Handel, "Hallelujah Chorus"
   https://youtu.be/BBZ7AfZR9xs

Pentatonix, "Evolution of Music"

https://youtu.be/GRyJu5gUIyY

Frankie Valli and the Four Seasons, "Sherry"

https://youtu.be/3pWBnodrR1M

"The Lion Sleeps Tonight" sung by The Tokens

https://youtu.be/zm0VAp4bkBA

"Do-Re-Mi" from the Sound of Music

https://youtu.be/YqCkkIGh9hQ

INSTRUMENT TIMBRE AND FAMILIES

Instruments fall into one of these four categories according to how their sound is produced.

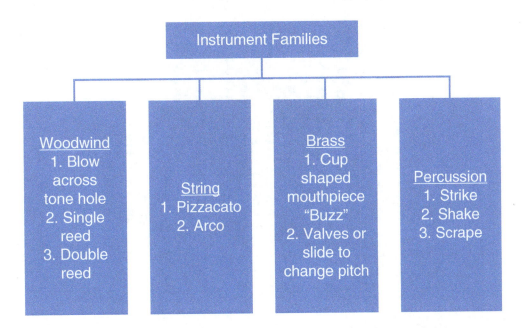

- Fill in this chart with the names of instruments from the symphony orchestra.

WOODWIND	STRING	BRASS	PERCUSSION

SYMPHONY ORCHESTRA SEATING CHART

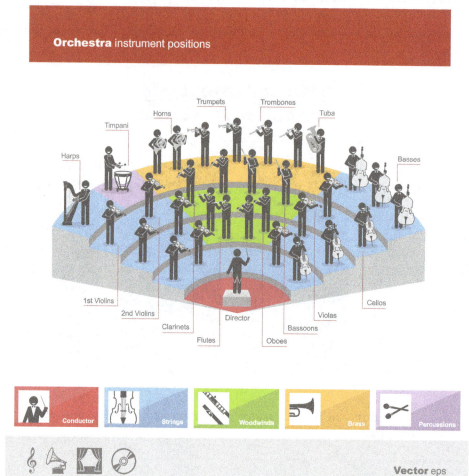

Orchestra instrument positions

- World Instrument Chart

Investigate instruments native to countries around the world and complete the chart below. Some instruments are listed in Chapter 4, Multi-Cultural, to get you started.

COUNTRY	NATIVE INSTRUMENT AND FAMILY
Japan	Koto/String

MUSIC USES THE EXPRESSIVE ELEMENT

The Expressive element is how you perform music; your awareness of how fast or slow, loud or quiet according to the style, mood and emotion expressed in the piece.

1. Tempo is the Italian word for how fast or how slow the beat of the music should be played. Italian is the universal language used for directions on how the music is to be performed.

    - Write the English word for these Italian tempos:

Grave _____

Largo _____

Adagio _____

Andante _____

Moderato _____

Allegro _____

Presto _____

Prestissimo _____

    - Read the tale of "The Tortoise and the Hare" and use instruments to enhance the fast and slow parts of the story. I.E. Use rhythm sticks to play a fast running tempo every time the Hare is mentioned. This is called a sound story.

What children's tale do you think would make an interesting sound story? Why?

_____

_____

2. Dynamics describe how loud or soft the music sounds.

   • Translate these Italian dynamic words into English.

Pianissimo _____

Piano _____

Mezzo Piano _____

Mezzo Forte _____

Forte _____

Fortissimo _____

   • Listen to the opening excerpt or the second movement of Haydn's "Surprise" Symphony No. 94 and describe the surprise you hear. https://youtu.be/VOLy6JxEDLw

_____

_____

What rhythm do you hear repeated?

_____

_____

TIP BOX

In Haydn's day, musicians depended on the largesse of rich patrons to support their livelihood. One of Haydn's patrons had a habit of falling asleep during performances, so Haydn came up with a creative solution!

   • Sing "Grizzly Bear" or "The Old Gray Cat". Music games can also reinforce Tempo and Dynamic concepts.

Describe the expressive elements used in the song.

_____

_____

3. Listen to "In the Hall of the Mountain King" and describe what you hear happening with the tempo and dynamics.

   • Tempo _____

Look up and define these tempo terms:

Accelerando _____

Ritardando _____

Fermata _____

   • Dynamics _____

Look up and define these additional dynamic terms.

Crescendo _____

Decrescendo _____

Now listen to the song, "Hair Up!" from the movie, TROLLS.

What familiar music theme do you hear?

_____

Compare/Contrast the two music selections using this Venn Diagram.

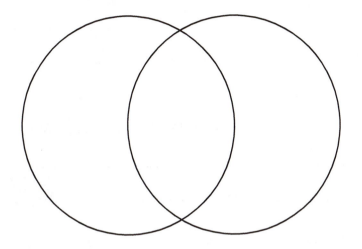

MUSIC HAS FORM

- A **phrase** is a musical sentence.
- A **section** of music has many phrases, like a paragraph has many sentences with one thought. Sections are labeled A, B, etc.
- A **song** can have one or more sections.
- Music can also have an **introduction** (preparing you to sing), an **interlude** between sections (can also be labeled a bridge) and a **coda** (Italian for a special ending).
- Larger pieces of music, like a symphony, have **movements**.

Five Common Forms in Elementary Children's Music with Examples

1. Echo
   Down by the Bay
   My Aunt Came Back

2. Call/response
   John, the Rabbit
   Train Is a—Comin'

3. Verse/refrain   Sections A B
   Jingle Bells
   Rocky Mountain
   Wild Horseman by Schumann

4. Rondo   Sections A B A C A
   "La Raspa"
   "Symphonie de Contours "
   Beethoven—"Rondo Alla Turca"

5. Theme and variations
    Mozart's "A Vous Direz-Vous, Maman"
    Benjamin Britten's "Young Person's Guide To the Orchestra"
    Charles Ives "Variations on America"

    • Select and sing several songs. Find the phrases, sections and name the form.

Title _____

Number of Phrases _____ Number of Sections _____ Form _____

Title _____

Number of Phrases _____ Number of Sections _____ Form _____

Title _____

Number of Phrases _____ Number of Sections _____ Form _____

MUSIC HAS STYLE

There are many musical styles; classical symphony, folk, rock, jazz, ragtime, blues, rhythm and blues, reggae, swing, heavy metal, gospel, Latin, country western, disco, boogie woogie, hymn, electronic, rap, Broadway musical, opera, military march, dixieland, new age. What other styles would you add? _____
Which are your favorites? _____

MUSICAL TIME PERIODS AND REPRESENTATIVE COMPOSERS

Medieval: An era of Western music including liturgical music used for the church as in Gregorian chants and secular troubador music of the 13th and 14th centuries. Composers include Guillame de Machaut, Hildegard von Bingen, Francesco Landini,

Renaissance: This era was from the 1400 to the 1500s. Music was mostly composed for the church and courtly life. Composers include Josquin Des Prez, William Byrd, Claudio Monteverdi, and Guillaume DuFay.

Baroque: This era was from 1600 to 1750. This music was very expressive and more elaborate than previous eras. Composers include J.S. Bach, G.F. Handel, Vivaldi, and Corelli.

Classical: This era was from 1750 to 1830. Music became the standard with which we are more familiar today following common principles, that is, the symphony form became standardized. Composers include Mozart, Joseph Haydn, and Muzio Clementi.

Romantic: This era overlaps from the late 1700s to the 1800s. Beethoven is considered a bridge from Classical to Romantic. The Romantic era focused on emotions and celebrated nature and beauty. Composers include Ludwig van Beethoven, Pytor Tchaikovsky, Robert Schumann, Clara Schumann, Franz Schubert, Franz Liszt, Frederic Chopin, and Giacomo Puccini.

Nationalistic: From the 1800s forward, Nationalistic Music uses ideas that are associated and identified with specific countries and ethnic groups. It often contains folk tunes. Composers include Edvard Grieg, Anton Dvorak, Smetana, and Leos Janacek.

Impressionistic: This era was from the late 1800s through the 20th century. This music suggests mood and emotion. Composers include Claude Debussy, Maurice Ravel, and Amy Beach.

20th–21st Centuries: This time period develops a diverse range of musical styles. Experimenting with new rhythms, chords and forms became common.

Transitional composers include Paul Hindemith, Sergi Prokofiev, Igor Stravinsky, Aaron Copland, Amy Beach, Lili Boulanger, Nadia Boulanger, Lili Boulanger, Dimitri Shostakovich, Astor Piazzolla, Alberto Ginastera, Heitor Villa-Lobos, Joaquin Rodrigo, Arturo Respighi, and Scott Joplin.

Jazz composers include Charlie Parker, Thelonius Monk, Miles Davis, Duke Ellington, John Coltrane, Dizzy Gillespie, Herbie Hancock, Charlie Mingus, Ella Fitzgerald, Billie Holiday, and Toshiko Akiyoshi.

Modern composers include Alban Berg, Arnold Schoenberg, Karlheinz Stockhausen, Luciano Berio, Charles Ives, Elliott Carter, Bela Bartok, William Grant Still, Margaret Bonds Leonard Bernstein and Ferde Grofe.

Current composers include Libby Larson, John Adams, Marcella Rodriguez, Enrico Chapela, Yihan Chen, Gabriela Ortiz, Tan Dun, Terri Lynn Carrington, Daniel Bernard Roumain, Anthony Davis, Anthony Braxton, Jonathan Bailey Holland, David Ashley White, Sharon Joy, and John Williams.

If you could live in another music time period, which one would you choose and why?

_____

_____

Application

1. Young Person's Guide to the Orchestra by Benjamin Britten

Thank you to our music teacher friend, Dr. Erin Hansen, for sharing this music worksheet.

- Listen to the Kohlner Orchestra https://youtu.be/4vbvhU22uAM and fill in the two-page worksheet, found in Appendix D.

2. Listening to and Analyzing Music

Listen to various musical selections from the list below and analyze them in reference to the 7 music elements. Fill in the worksheet.

- "In The Hall of the Mountain King" by Edvard Grieg
- "William Tell Overture" by Gioachino Rossini
- "March of the Toreadors" by Georges Bizet
- "The Syncopated Clock " by Leroy Anderson
- "Also Spracht Zarathustra" by Richard Strauss

TIP BOX

The Young Person's Guide to the Orchestra is an example of an English Language Arts cross-curricular lesson for Grade 5 TEKS. Students understand new vocabulary and use it when reading and writing.

- "The Arabian Dance" by Pyotr Tchaikovsky
- "Can Can Music" by Jacques Offenbach

ANALYZING MUSIC TEMPLATE

1. Music title, composer _____

Rhythm—meter, rhythm patterns _____
Melody—melodic contour, high, low, repeated, skips, leaps _____
Expressive elements—tempo, dynamics (Italian abbrev.), _____
Crescendo, decrescendo, fermata _____
Timbre—families of instruments _____
Solo, groups, voice classification: _____
Form—AB (Verse/Refrain), A1A2A3 (Theme and Variations), ABACA (Rondo), _____

Musical style: _____
Texture—monophonic, homophonic, polyphonic _____
Harmony—unison, call and response, echo song, round/canon, partner song, descant, harmony _____

2. Music title, composer _____

Rhythm—meter, rhythm patterns _____
Melody—melodic contour, high, low, repeated, skips, leaps _____
Expressive elements—tempo, dynamics (Italian abbrev.), _____
Crescendo, decrescendo, fermata, _____
Timbre—families of instruments _____
Solo, groups, voice classification: _____
Form—AB (Verse/Refrain), A1A2A3 (Theme and Variations), ABACA (Rondo), _____

Musical style: _____
Texture—monophonic, homophonic, polyphonic _____
Harmony—unison, call and response, echo song, round/canon, partner song, descant, harmony _____

3. Music title, composer _____

Rhythm—meter, rhythm patterns _____
Melody—melodic contour, high, low, repeated, skips, leaps _____
Expressive elements—tempo, dynamics (Italian abbrev.), _____
Crescendo, decrescendo, fermata _____
Timbre—families of instruments _____
Solo, groups, voice classification: _____
Form—AB (Verse/Refrain), A1A2A3 (Theme and Variations), ABACA (Rondo), _____

Musical style: _____
Texture—monophonic, homophonic, polyphonic _____
Harmony—unison, call and response, echo song, round/canon, partner song, descant, harmony _____

4. Music title, composer _____

Rhythm—meter, rhythm patterns _____
Melody—melodic contour, high, low, repeated, skips, leaps _____
Expressive elements—tempo, dynamics (Italian abbrev.), _____
Crescendo, decrescendo, fermata _____
Timbre—families of instruments _____
Solo, groups, voice classification: _____
Form—AB (Verse/Refrain), A1A2A3 (Theme and Variations), ABACA (Rondo),

_____

Musical style: _____
Texture—monophonic, homophonic, polyphonic _____
Harmony—unison, call and response, echo song, round/canon, partner song, descant, harmony _____

LISTENING MAP

For a multi-sensory experience, listening maps are sometimes used to provide a visual and tactile focus while hearing the music. A Listening Map is an artistic representation of what you hear in the music. It can be in different shapes (follow the symbols left to right, top to bottom, or be a pathway that students follow). It can have pictures that are abstract or literal to coordinate with the culture or subject.

Listening Maps should be colorful, interesting, and guide students to engage with the music by touching each symbol in order as the music plays. One symbol may represent a section of music, a phrase, or individual beats, but the map must be consistent and easy to follow.

Listening Maps should emphasize one music element to reinforce the student's learning. When you review listening maps on line, you will notice the most common elements depicted are rhythm, form and timbre. Expressive symbols are also frequently added.

Listening Map Assignment

Create an artistic, educational, and accurate visual guide to be used with a musical excerpt 1—2 minutes in length. Focus in on one music element that the music demonstrates. Display your visual as a projected image, handout, or as a large chart which can be seen clearly by all students in the class.

Lead the class through your visual guide while playing the excerpt of your musical selection. Read the rubric for additional requirements needed for your map.

MORE LISTENING SELECTIONS

Olympic Fanfare by Leo Renaud
Gayane/Sabre Dance by Aram Khachaturian
Trepak/Russian Dance from the Nutcracker by Pyotr Tchaikovsky
Chinese Dance from the Nutcracker by Pyotr Tchaikivsky
Jamaican Rhumba by Arthur Benjamin
Hoedown by Aaron Copland

Variations on America by Charles Ives
Surprise Symphony by Joseph Haydn
The Carnival of the Animals by Camille Saint-Saens
Eine Kleine Nachtmusik by Wolfgang Mozart
Pictures at an Exhibition by Modest Mussorgsky
Peter and the Wolf by Sergei Prokofiev
Flight of the Bumblebee by Nikolai Rimsky-Korsakov
Danse Macabre by Camille Saint-Saens
Washington Post March by John Phillip Sousa
Stars and Stripes Forever by John Phillip Sousa
Fanfare for the Common Man by Aaron Copland
On the Trail by Ferde Grofe from The Grand Canyon Suite
Little Train of Caipira by Villa-Lobos
String Quartet in E Flat Major by Franz Schubert
The Planets by Gustav Holst
Peer Gynt Suite by Edvard Grieg
Blue Danube Waltz by Johann Strauss II
Minuet in G by J. S. Bach
The Four Seasons by Antonio Vivaldi
Canon in D by Johann Pachelbel

RUBRIC FOR LISTENING MAP ASSIGNMENT

Student _____

Recording quality. Length 1–2 minutes
Heading: Title and Composer
Educational Value of Music
Visual Creativity: Artistic, Engaging, Colorful
Visual Accurate representation of the music
Key defining symbols
Visual Large enough for all to see (chart, Power Point, Handout)
Musical element(s): _____
Presentation skills

Why do you think music listening activities are important for children to experience?

_____

_____

Chapter Reflection List below the music activity and/or song used in this chapter to connect MUSIC with another elementary subject.

MUSIC ACTIVITY AND/OR SONG:	OBJECTIVE: GRADE LEVEL
ELA	
Science	
Social Studies	
Math	
Health/PE	
Theatre/Art	

ENGAGING CHILDREN WITH MOVEMENT

CHAPTER 7

Through movement children can develop their imagination and creative gifts. Moving to music helps in the discovery and understanding of musical concepts, such as discovering the body can create images. Moving with freedom can increase self-image and strengthens coordination and spatial awareness. Movement also develops a common vocabulary that can be transferred from one style of dance to another regardless of culture or time period.

© Cherry-Merry/Shutterstock.com

Chapter Objectives

After completing this chapter, you will be able to:

- Experience various movement activities and relate them to musical elements.
- Use movement vocabulary correctly while teaching a movement activity.

Vocabulary

Types of Movement

Locomotor Movement—Movement done while traveling through shared space.

LOCOMOTOR MOVEMENT		
• Walk	• Skip	• Hop
• Tip-toe	• Side-close	• Sashay
• March	• Slide	• Strut
• Stomp	• Jog	• Sauntering
• Run	• Forward/backward	• Strolling
• Gallop	• In/out	

Nonlocomoter Movement—Movement that does not move through space, movement is done in place.

NON LOCOMOTOR MOVEMENT		
• King Tut	• Hitch Hike	• Scissors
• March in Place	• Knock Knees	• Airplane Wings
• Jump	• Shrug shoulders	• Windshield Wipers
• Lassos	• Tap Shoulders	• Twist
• Arm Roll	• Chicken Wings	• Click Heels
• Sway	• Stretch	• Bend/Straighten
• Karate Kick	• Slash	• Head Nod

© Africa Studio/Shutterstock.com

Body Percussion—It can be added to nonlocomotor and locomotor movements:

• Snap	• Clap	• Pat	• Stomp	• Click Tongue

Pathways—Ways for children to move throughout shared space.

- Circle—moving counter clockwise
- Straight—moving forward, backward and/or diagonally
- Zigzag—crooked/jagged
- Curved—snake
- Figure eight

Levels—The movements and pathways mentioned can be performed at various levels (high, middle, low, and in between). Levels can be performed with various urgencies/intensities such as strong, weak, and in between. Tempo is another factor to consider when performing movement.

DIRECTIONAL FACINGS		
• Face to face	• Shoulder to shoulder	• Face down
• Side to side	• Head to head	
• Back to back	• Face up	

Skill Development

TRANSFER IMAGES TO MOVEMENT

Create situations for children to practice movements that imitate things they see around them, stories they have read or music that they interpret.

- Encourage your students to pretend they are a/an:

Bird flying
Giant stomping
Wind-blown tree
Ice Skater

"Carnival of the Animals"—Music Element: Expressive, Rhythm

- Play selections from "Carnival of the Animals" by Camille Saint-Saens and let children march and strut like a lion, hop like a kangaroo, swim like a fish, etc.

- Listening Selection: *Aquarium from Carnival of the Animals* by C. Saint-Saens.

1. Have students seated on the floor. Explain that the A section sounds like fish swimming and play an excerpt of that section. Explain that the B section sounds like it could be a beautiful coral reef. Imagine the seaweed waving in the water and the bubbles flowing to the surface as you listen to an excerpt of this section.
2. Hand each student a scarf. Explore movements for the A section, then for the B section.
3. Find a partner, decide who will be the fish (A) and who will be the coral reef (B). As the music plays, partners perform their movements during their sections and freeze when it is not their turn.

TIP BOX

Teachers can show children pictures or videos of a variety of movements they have not previously experienced. Example, frogs hopping, birds flying or people snow skiing. This can help them imitate and be more creative with their movement.

DIRECTIONAL FACINGS AND LEVELS

"Hey There, Let's Go!"—Music Element: Expressive Elements, Rhythm, Texture

1. Teacher chooses a music selection. "Russian Melody" by Del Castilo (which has a "Hey!" in the music) works well for this activity. Any music with even phrases from classical to pop tunes are also good choices.
2. Teacher reviews level possibilities: high, medium, low; and pathways: straight, curved, etc.
3. Students think to themselves and plan to travel to three different locations making a pathway and level choice for each section of travel.
4. Have students tell their plan to a neighbor.
5. Teacher plays music and children begin moving.

Optional: Students change pathway and level choices at a sound cue from the teacher using a triangle or a drum.

TIP BOX

Have half of the students move to the side and observe while the other half performs. The observers silently choose a person to watch. After the performance the observers tell whom they were watching and identify the directional pathways and levels they performed.

© Oksana Shyfrych/Shutterstock.com

MUSIC GAMES

Combining singing with movement to play a game becomes the ultimate fun. These kinds of games are traditionally called play party games. In addition to being fun, they reinforce rhythm and melody elements. Teachers could use these games for rainy day recess, transitional or re-focusing activities, celebrations or the integration of music with social studies and physical education.

Freeze Game—Music Element: Rhythm

1. Choose a recording with a very peppy tempo. Tell students to improvise loco-motor movement to the music and say they must freeze when the music stops at random times.
2. Students sit down if they continue to move after the music stops. They become part of the judges who spot people who wiggle and move on the next pause.
3. Keep going until all but three children are left and all begin again.

Optional: Students can rejoin the game by trading places with someone they spot moving.

"Old King Glory"—Music Element: Rhythm, Melody

1. Teach the song by Rote method. Have the class form one large circle.
2. While singing, walk the beat counterclockwise with a leader walking the opposite direction outside the circle,
3. The leader taps the three people he walks behind on the words, "the first one, the second one, the third follow me." Those three join the leader walking in the opposite direction.
4. Continue until all but one student is left in the original circle. That student could begin the next game.

Shadow Dancing—Music Element: Rhythm, Expressive Element

1. Divide students into pairs. Choose one person to be the first leader.
2. Teacher plays music selections with various tempos and moods. The leader creates locomotor movements while the partner "shadows" or mirrors the movement.
3. At the sound cue from the teacher, (triangle, drum, etc.) the other student becomes the leader. Encourage children to be very expressive with their movements, responding to the mood, tempo, and dynamics of the music.

Optional: Give children a prop such as a bean bag, ribbon stick, puppet or scarf to help them create movements.

See Appendix A for these other fun music games:
"Little Johnny Brown","Jump Jim Joe","Se, Se, Se", "Grizzly Bear", "The Old Gray Cat", "Here We Go Looby Loo", "Circle Round the Zero", Draw Me a Bucket of Water", "Apple Tree", "Hunt the Cows", "We Are Playing in the Forest", "Pizza, Pizza Daddy-O", "Here Come a Bluebird", "Miss Mary Mack", "Charlie Over the Ocean", "Chicken On the Fencepost", "Juba"

FAVORITE GROUP DANCE SUGGESTIONS

Folk and modern dance movements can be just as much fun as a music game. For more information and directions look in Appendix A and B or for videos and demonstrations on line.

- Favorite Group Dance Suggestions

© Aleutie/Shutterstock.com

Line Dances: "I Love a Rainy Night", "Pata, Pata", "Cotton Eyed Joe", "Boot Scootin' Boogie", "Alabama Gal"

© Kobby Dagan/Shutterstock.com

TIP BOX

Rainy Day Recess is more fun using movement. Have one of these resources on hand:

- "Kids in Action" and "Kids in Motion" by Greg and Steve have several selections for guided movement and are a good resource for teachers.

http://www.gregand steve.com/Activity-Books_c_21.html

- "Jump Jim Joe" , "Sashay the Donut", "Down in the Valley", "Chimes of Dunkirk", "Rise Sally Rise", "Listen to the Mockingbird" by New England Dancing Masters are a wonderful set of CD/Books/Videos for teachers.

http:// dancingmasters.com/

- Don't miss looking at Robert Amchin and his teaching videos on You Tube:

https://www.youtube. com/user/Robamchin

- Artie Almeida has many creative music ideas. Check out her web site:

http://www. artiealmeida.com/

Circle Dances with Partners—Mixers: "La Raspa", "Fjaskern", "Patty Cake Polka" "Troika"

Circle Dances with No Partners: "Farandole", "Zemer Atik", "Chicken Dance"
Open Circle Dance: "Ya Abud"

Longways Sets: "Virginia Reel", "Jefferson Reel","Yankee Doodle" contradance, "Grand March"

Square Dances: "Trail of the Lonesome Pine", "Listen to the Mockingbird"

Applications:

1. "Scarf Movement"

Music: "Aquarium" from Carnival of Animals by Camille Saint Saens
Music Element: Melody
Activity directions:
Use your scarf and your body to show what you hear in the melody.
Move in the room in an S or Figure 8 pattern, moving the scarf expressively.
No talking while you are demonstrating what you hear.

Circle the 3 correct music terms that were demonstrated.

• Form	• Texture	• Melodic direction
• Body levels	• Pathways	• Harmony

Teach a Movement Lesson Assignment

You will be placed in a group in class and given directions for a movement (patterned dance) lesson with music. Your group will have 20 minutes to plan how to present the lesson to the class. Make sure everyone in your group participates. Points awarded for accuracy in deciphering the lesson plan, clarity of your directions and success of the class in doing the dance.

Name two of your favorite movement activities. _____

_____

Why do you think music movement activities are important for children to experience?

_____

_____

Lesson Plan Example for Movement

Music Element: Form
Exploring Directional Facings and Vertical Levels in Space Creating a Movement Form for Upper Elementary

MUSIC TEKS: Creative Expression: §117.115.
The student performs movement alone and with others to a varied repertoire of music using gross motor, fine motor, locomotor, and non-locomotor skills and integrated movement such as hands and feet moving together.

Specific Objective: The student will create locomotor and non-locomotor movements demonstrating different forms (ABA; AB; Rondo).

Materials: Any even phrased music, pop tunes, as well as classical ones are good for this activity. Music used today: *Happy* by P. Williams; Lyle Lovett's *That Right You're Not from Texas, But Texas Wants You Anyway.*

Procedures:

Number these steps in the procedures:

1. Discuss, show and notate locomotor movements. List on the board.
2. Use a variety of non-locomotor movements; change by phrase, to music. Have the students cue for phrase changes.
3. Discuss and show non-locomotor movements.
4. Have the students plan silently which three locomotor movements they will use. Now say the plan aloud. Use a sound cue for phrase changes.
5. Alternate by 16 beat phrases a non-locomotor movement with a locomotor movement to the same music.
6. Discuss the form possibilities mentioned above.
7. Divide into groups to create a movement form.
8. Perform pieces.

TIP BOX

Make a separate category for body percussion: clap, snap, stomp.

Have half of the students move to the side and observe while the other half performs. The observers silently choose a person to watch. After the performance the observers tell whom they were watching and identify the movements they performed.

When presenting dance, have the students watch the step or listen to the language (not numbers/count) for the step first. Then have them verbalize the step before doing the step. Example: forward, forward, forward, forward; side/close, side/close. This gives students time to process the information.

Perform pieces. Have the students/audience identify the movements used after each performance.

Assessment: To what extent and artistry level (master, apprentice, novice) was the student able to achieve the objective? Are the students able to identify the types of movements used in each piece?

Chapter Reflection: List below the music activity and/or song used in this chapter to connect MUSIC with another elementary subject.

MUSIC ACTIVITY AND/OR SONG:	OBJECTIVE: GRADE LEVEL
ELA	
Science	
Social Studies	
Math	
Health/PE	
Theatre/Art	

LESSON PLANNING

There are two main methods used in teaching songs: Rote method and Note (notation) method.

Chapter Objectives

After completing this chapter, you will be able to:

- Create a lesson plan.
- Teach a simple song using the ROTE method.
- Teach an upper elementary song using the NOTE method.

LESSON PLAN DIRECTIONS

Lesson Plans help a teacher to think ahead globally and specifically on what can be accomplished with students in the time allotted. Substitutes will need the details and Principals/Curriculum Supervisors are required to know exactly what is being taught, how it is being taught and how it is being assessed. A good lesson plan should be helpful to the teacher to streamline presentations and to use time efficiently for the students. The following sections should be included.

Your Name:
Grade Level:
National Music Standard or Music TEKS Objective: This is the overall state mandated goal for your lesson. The National Music Standards can be found on line. The Texas Essential Knowledge and Skills (TEKS) list is found on the Texas Education Agency website. Copy and paste the Music TEKS objective on your lesson plan.

Specific Objective: This is your specific goal for this particular lesson where you decide what it is you want to teach. Focus on the skill you will assess. Although other information may be taught in a supporting way, that is not the FOCUS for this lesson and does not need an objective.

Materials: List everything you will use to teach this lesson; what <u>you</u> will need and what a substitute would need to teach the lesson competently.

Process: These are the step by step, very detailed directions of how you will present the lesson. You may use a bullet/listing format, numbers, etc. Always identify the opening engagement of the students or "Hook," assessment, and closure portions of the process.

- To engage the learner relate your new information to previous learning or "hook" their interest in what you are about to teach. Let children discuss these connections. "Remember yesterday when we were writing poems with rhyming words? Today I have a fun song with rhyming words." or "Yesterday we started discussing the Revolutionary War. Today let's sing 'Yankee Doodle' and find descriptions of life in an Army camp in the lyrics."
- List the step-by-step directions teaching the content of the lesson.
- List what the assessment will be for evaluation.
- The Closure/Extension portion is the last part of your lesson and it is important to relate it to future learning. It is also important to restate what the objective of the lesson was and to encourage children to verbally say what they learned. Making learning connections in the brain is very valuable to the students. "Next time we sing this song we are going to play a game that children played over 100 years ago." or "I imagine we can create new verses to this song with rhyming words next time we get together to sing."

Assessment: Even though the assessment is included in procedures, make it a separate category for the Principal/ curriculum director to get a quick look at evaluation. This is a restatement of the specific objective. How will you know the students have achieved the objective for the lesson?

Ways to evaluate: By listening/aural; by seeing/visual; by testing/pencil & paper; etc.

What is your prediction of success based on past knowledge and the students in this subject area? Choose one of the following: Mastery 98–100% of students; Intermediate 90–97% of students; Novice 80–89% of students.

There are two main methods used in teaching songs: Rote method and Note Method.

ROTE METHOD TEACHING GUIDELINES

Choose the rote method to teach a song or a part of a song that is short, repetitive, and easy to learn. The teacher has the song memorized and uses an "echo me" technique. It is very important for the teacher to sing tunefully so the children have a good model to follow. Students do not look at printed music.

These guidelines are the basic steps in the Process/Procedure section of a lesson plan.

1. Focus the students' attention by asking a specific question they answer after you sing the entire song. "Listen to my song and tell me

_____ "

2. Children listen to the teacher sing the whole song while keeping a quiet, steady beat on their laps. Get the answers to your question.

3. If the song is more complicated, ask a second question to focus attention and sing again. Get answers to your questions.

TIP BOX

Teachers should include live presentations, pictures, etc., to enhance and expose children to images they have not previously experienced. Connect animal movement with books such as the "Pete the Cat" series.

TIP BOX

A cue:
- Tells when to start singing.
- Tells the tempo to sing.
- Gives the pitch to start singing.

4. T. points to self and sings first phrase of the song.
5. T. points to head and S. audiate. [internalizing; singing it in your head before singing aloud.]
6. T. points to S. to sing phrase aloud. Teacher does not sing along.
7. Continue for each phrase.
8. T. combines two phrases and repeats process.
9. T. gives singing cue and sings whole song with students. Singing cue: "READY< SING" on the starting pitch.
10. T. gives singing cue and S. sing tunefully from memory without the teacher. This is the Assessment.

ROTE METHOD LESSON PLAN EXAMPLE

Song: Lil' Liza Jane

Name: _____

Grade Level: 2nd

National Music Standard: Singing, alone and with others, a varied repertoire of music. Or **2nd Grade Music TEKS:** 117. 109 (3) Creative expression. The student performs a varied repertoire of developmentally appropriate music in informal or formal settings. The student is expected to:

(A) sing tunefully or play classroom instruments, including rhythmic and melodic patterns, independently or in groups;

Specific Objective: Students will sing the song "Lil' Liza Jane" tunefully from memory.

Materials:

- A copy of the notation for the teacher.
- A recording of the song for the teacher.
- Pitch source.

Process:

1. **Engaging learners:** T. "When we learned the story of "The Star Spangled Banner" yesterday, we learned about Fort McHenry and the city Baltimore, Maryland. Today, I have a new song about that city and a girl who lives in it. Listen to my song and tell me her name."
2. T. asks S. to keep a beat on their leg during the song, gets the starting pitch, and sings song. Ask for answers (Liza Jane).
3. Listen to my song again, keeping the beat, and listen for the direction of the melody at the end of the song.
4. T. sings and asks for answers.
5. T. points to self and sings first phrase.
6. T. points to head for S. to audiate*. [*audiate: internalizing; singing it in your head before singing aloud.]
7. S. sing phrase aloud (T. does not sing along).
8. T. continues for each phase of the song.
9. T. points to self and sings two phrases together.

TIP BOX

For reteaching or further reinforcement, optional steps:

- T. splits class in half. Group one sings the first half of the song. Teacher gives singing cue for the students to start.
- T. lifts a hand for the Group Two to sing the second half of the song.
- Now switch and let the second half start the song. Teacher gives the singing cue for the students to start.
- Optional step: T. sings part of the phrase and S. fill in the blank singing the rest of the phrase. Continue for the whole song.

1. Assessment: Teacher gives the singing cue for the students to sing the whole song by themselves. T. listens for tuneful singing.
2. Closure: Review what was learned and connect to future learning.

10. S. audiate, then sing aloud.
11. Continue same for the rest of the two phrases together.
12. T. sings the Cue and leads the class in singing the whole song.
13. Optional step: Split the class in half.
14. Have half of the class sing the first half of the song. T. sings the Cue to start.
15. T. lifts a hand for the other half to sing the second half of the song.
16. Now switch and let the second half start the song. T. sings the Cue to start.
    • Optional step: T. sings part of the phrase, and S. fill in the blank singing the rest of the phrase. Continue for the whole song.
17. **Assess:** T. cues the S. to sing the whole song by themselves. T. listens for tuneful singing.
18. **Closure**: T. says, "Very good job singing all the correct pitches, rhythms and lyrics! Tomorrow when we meet we will add movement steps to our song."

Assessment: Students performed the song "Lil Liza Jane" tunefully from memory.

Application

ROTE METHOD TEACHING ASSIGNMENT

This assignment is designed to provide you with experience teaching a K, 1st/2nd-grade song using the rote method and emphasizing the music fundamentals of rhythm and pitch. You will be given 5 minutes to teach the song to the class.

This assignment has three parts:

• Lesson Plan—Construct a plan for teaching your assigned song.
• Teaching the Lesson—Use the evaluation form found in Appendix D. Please fill out the top portion (name/song) and bring the evaluation form to class on the day you are scheduled to teach.
• Self-evaluation—This evaluation is used to self assess your teaching.

RUBRIC FOR ROTE METHOD TEACHING ASSIGNMENT

Song Introduction/Engagement of Students
Appropriate Range, Starting Pitch
Song memorization
Tuneful singing
Correct Rhythm and Lyrics
Clear Directions and Leadership
Rote Process
Effective Cue
Specific Feedback to Students
Addressing accuracy/re-teaching
Closure
Pacing/Energy Level

NOTE TEACHING METHOD GUIDELINES

Choose the note method to teach a longer, more complicated song, usually to older students. Here the teacher and the students see the music notation and lyrics via Book, Smartboard, Power Point, etc. Use a quality recording of children's voices that are in the appropriate range.

These guidelines are the basic steps in the Process section of a lesson plan.

1. Engage the students by connecting to previous learning or experiences.
2. T. points out specific music concepts that will aid the students in singing the song.
   * Expressive Element Symbols—dynamics, tempo
   * Melodic Contour—leaps, skips, repeated notes
   * Music Symbols—repeat signs, 1st and 2nd endings, coda, fermata, etc.
   * Form—verse, refrain
   * Rhythm Elements—repeated patterns
   * Harmony—chords, ostinato, descant
   * Timbre—instrument parts to play
3. Lead the students in listening to one verse of the song or part of the song.
   * Ask a question to be answered after listening to the song or a portion of the song to help focus S. attention. Get answers.
   * Discuss what was heard in relation to Guideline #2.
4. Lead students in singing the song with the recording.
   * Sing out as the leader.
   * Give a CUE during musical introduction as to when to begin singing.
5. Assess singing. Briefly, go over places where they may have had difficulty.
6. Lead in singing the song again.
7. Add planned movement or planned instrument patterns.
   * Teach in small sections, practicing each part and adding more and more until it is complete.
   * Write out your instrument/movement plan in the lesson plan in detail.
   * Make your plan complex for 3rd–5th-grade students.
   * Use Power Point visuals to teach quickly and to keep your lesson in sequential order.
   * Have your materials (instruments, scarves, props, etc.) ready to use as you begin teaching.
   * To continue singing the song, assign a few students to sing while others do the instrument/movement patterns. Plan to rotate students so everyone experiences each part.
8. Assess: End with a complete, best final performance, assessing instruments/movement plan.
9. Closure:
   * Restate what was learned in the lesson.
   * Connect to future learning/Extension ideas.

TIP BOX

* The quality of the recording is very important. It should have good models of children's voices and quality instrumental parts.

* Look at your students, make eye contact and encourage them to sing.

* Remind students of good singing posture/skills.

* Give positive, specific feedback.

SAMPLE LESSON PLAN NOTE METHOD TEACHING

Song: The Rattlin' Bog
Name: _____
Grade 4
National Music Standard:

1. Singing, alone and with others, a varied repertoire of music.
2. Performing on instruments, alone and with others, a varied repertoire of music.

Music TEKS Objectives:
117.15 (2) Creative Expression/Performance. The student is expected to (A) sing or play a classroom instrument tunefully, independently or in groups.
      (If doing Movement)
117.15 (C) move alone and with others to a varied repertoire of music using gross motor, fine motor, locomotor, and nonlocomotor skills and integrated movement such as hands and feet moving together.

Science TEKS Objectives:
112.15 (b) Knowledge and skills (7) Earth and Space. The students know that earth consists of useful resources. The student is expected to (A) examine properties of soils, including color and texture, capacity to retain water and ability to support the growth of plants.

Specific Objectives:

1. The student will sing the song "The Rattlin' Bog" tunefully.
2. The student will play an instrument pattern with correct pitches and rhythms. (opt. for Movement—The student will demonstrate the movement pattern correctly.)
3. The student will explain/define Bog, Valley Bog, and Rattlin' Bog terms.

Materials: Pictures of: selected instruments, an Irish Bog, a valley bog, the words in the song (Tree, Limb, Branch, Nest, Egg, Bird) and a world map.
   A copy of the notation for the teacher and students.
   A quality CD recording of the song, preferably with children's voices.
   Instruments: Boomwhacker pitches for the F and C chords, hand drums, glockenspiel, finger cymbals, triangle, wood block, cabasa and guiro.

Procedures:

1. Introduction: Show pictures of Ireland, map and bogs. Review science information previously learned about a bog as a specific wetland habitat (peat layers with moisture to create bogs.)
2. Tell students dried squares of peat from a bog can be burned for fuel in homes. Now many bog areas are being preserved as endangered wetlands. Today, we are going to sing a folk song from Ireland about a special bog—a "Rattlin' Bog." Have a student locate Ireland on the world map.

3. Look in your music books at the song "Rattlin' Bog" and find the word refrain. Listen for where this bog is located. Play the refrain and get answer. (In the valley-O)

4. Play the refrain again and ask students to sing along with the CD. Remind students to sit tall, open mouth, breathe, etc. and cue students when to sing. Give specific positive feedback.

5. Point to the picture of the bog on the board. Describe a valley bog where a stream runs through the peat in the low part of a valley.

6. Ask what kind of bog are we singing about? Sing the refrain again and get answer (rattlin' bog). Describe a rattlin' bog as one where the peat floats on top of the stream water in the valley and shakes or "rattles" as you walk across it.

7. Let's sing the first verse and find out what is growing in the "rattlin' bog. Show students where the verse is in the music. Continue to play the CD and cue students when to sing. Get answer (a tree). Place picture on the board.

8. This song has a fun trick to it. We are going to add items to the tree. Each time we add an item we sing the whole list. Show in the music how to follow the verses.

9. Let's sing the refrain and listen to the 2nd verse to see what is added to the tree. Play CD and cue students to sing. Get answer (limb) and place picture on the board.

10. Continue singing additional verses and adding items. Place pictures on the board. Use the pictures as a visual cue for the words if the students have trouble following the music. Practice singing these words cumulatively if needed.

11. Give specific positive feedback on singing. Say this type of song is a cumulative song because each verse adds one more item to our list for us to remember.

12. Sing the entire song without stopping and give feedback.

13. Instruments would be fun to add to our song. Place a picture of an instrument next to the picture of the cumulative words in the song. (Tree-wood block, Limb-guiro, branch-cabasa, nest-triangle, egg-finger cymbals, bird-glockenspiel glissando). Hand out these instruments, reminding students everyone will get a turn as we share. Tell students to play their instrument every time their word is sung. Practice saying words and having students play one time.

14. Let's add hand drums to the refrain. Hand out 3 or 4 and ask students to keep a light steady beat during the refrain only. Practice. (Optional: add a "Texas-Maine" (two eighths-quarter) rhythm on "Valley-O").

15. Sing song with CD and let students play while others sing.

16. If time permits, (optional) add Boomwhacker pitches for the F and C chords to play the refrain only, looking at the chord names above the music. Practice drums and BW together as students sing refrain.

17. Assessment: Sing again with all instruments.

18. If time permits, give other children a chance to play instruments.

19. Collect all instruments carefully and put them away as you give specific positive feedback to students. Ask for helpers to put away music books.

20. Assessment: Ask students to identify a bog, valley bog and rattlin' bog, using pictures as clues.

21. Closure: Next music time we can play our instruments and sing our fun song from Ireland. Now let's learn more about this special habitat. Take out your science books.

Movement Pattern (replace steps 13–19):

13. Have students line up in a longways set. (Two lines of partners facing each other about 8 feet apart.)
14. Refrain:

   a. Step forward Beats 1–4, clapping partner's hands on beat 4.
   b. Step back to place beats 5–8, clapping own hands in a "Texas-Maine" rhythm pattern while singing "Valley-O."
   c. Next 8 beats. Move forward to right elbow swing partner and return to place, clapping on "Valley-O."

15. Verses: Assign each pair of partners a specific movement for each key word to act out as it is sung. Always clap on "Valley-O." If there are more than seven sets of partners, have two pairs do one word together.

   a. Bog—Stomp feet as if walking through squishy mud.
   b. Tree—Do—Si—Do with partner.
   c. Limb—Two sets of partners form a right hand star and circle clockwise returning to place.
   d. Branch—Take two steps forward, hold arms like branches, and rattle back and forth. Step back in place.
   e. Nest—Partners join hands and circle right one time and step back in place.
   f. Egg—Partners step forward, arms above head in egg shape and twirl one time. Step back in place.
   g. Bird—Partners move arms as flying and go down the outside of the lines and return to place.

Assessment:

1. Are the students singing tunefully the song "The Rattlin' Bog"?
2. Are the students playing the instrument pattern with correct pitches and rhythms? OR Are the students demonstrating the movement pattern correctly?
3. Are students able to identify bog, valley bog, and rattlin' bog terms?

Application

NOTE METHOD TEACHING ASSIGNMENT

Choose an upper elementary (grade 3, 4, or 5) song that can also teach another elementary subject.

This assignment has three parts:

• Lesson Plan—Construct a cross-curricular plan. Include Music TEKS objectives as well as cross-curricular TEKS objectives. Although you will only teach the music sections of your lesson, show how the lesson would extend to another curriculum area and briefly describe those activities.

- Teaching the Lesson—Use a recording of the song as a demonstration and to aid in teaching the song. Teach your lesson plan, referencing the integrated connection in your introduction/conclusion. Visually, show the notation (power point, textbook, or handout) to aid in teaching the music elements of the song.
- Self-evaluation—This evaluation is used to self assess your teaching.

NOTE METHOD TEACHING ASSIGNMENT RUBRIC

Introduction/Engagement of Students
Effective use of Power Point
Integration/Cross-Curricular
Effective Use of Notation
Effective Singing w/CD
Effective Cueing
Effective Use of Movement/Instruments
Specific Positive Feedback
Addressing/Reteaching Student Learning
Clear Directions and Leadership
Pacing/Energy Level
Assessment
Closure

Chapter Reflection: List below the music activity and/or song used in this chapter to connect MUSIC with another elementary subject.

MUSIC ACTIVITY AND/OR SONG:	OBJECTIVE: GRADE LEVEL
ELA	
Science	
Social Studies	
Math	
Health/PE	
Theatre/Art	

MORE SAMPLE LESSONS

1.   **See Saw—Traditional Children's Song**

Grade Level: Kindergarten and/or 1st Grade
MUSIC TEKS: Foundations: Creative Expression. The student describes and analyzes musical sound; sing a well-known children's song.
Specific Objective: The students will sing See Saw and identify the highest pitch by placing their hands on their heads.
Materials: See Saw, bell set for retrieving starting pitch.
Process:

- Teacher asks students what is their favorite thing to do at a park (ride the swings, go on the merry-go-round, climb on the monkey bars, ride on the see-saw).
- Students follow teacher and keep a steady beat on their laps and listen for "How many different tones/pitches does the song have?" (2)
- T. sings See Saw and when finished asks "How many different tones . . . ."
- T. points to self and sings first phrase.
- T. points to head for S. to audiate (to sing internally not aloud).
- S. sing phrase aloud.
- T. sings the remaining phrase with S. audiating before singing aloud.
- Students show the two tones by placing the highest one on their head, the middle one on their shoulders. Students follow along with the teacher.
- Now sing without the teacher's help.

Assessment: The students will show, with 95% accuracy the highest pitch by placing their hands on their heads. Visual and aural observations.
Extension: On another day, students can learn the see-saw movements with a partner.

2.   **Rain Rain—Traditional Children's Song**

Grade Level: Kindergarten and/or 1st Grade
TEKS: Foundations: music literacy. The student describes and analyzes musical sound.
Specific Objective: The students will sing Rain Rain and identify the highest pitch by placing their hands on their heads.
Materials: Rain Rain, melody bells for retrieving starting pitch.
Process:

- Teacher asks students to make rain sounds using their fingers (snapping or tapping on the floor). "Can you make it rain, one drop at a time?" "Can you make it flood?"
- Students keep a steady beat on their laps and listen for "How many different tones/pitches does the song have?" (3)
- T. sings Rain Rain and when finished asks "How many different tones . . . ."
- T. points to self and sings first phrase.
- T. points to head for S. to audiate (to sing internally not aloud).
- S. sing phrase aloud
- T. sings the remaining phrases with S. audiating each phrase before singing aloud.

- Students show the three tones by placing the highest one on their head, the middle one on their shoulders and the lower one on their lap. Students follow along with the teacher.
- Students are asked to place their name in "Little Johnny wants to play."
- Students are asked to sing Rain Rain and place the pitches on their body: head, shoulders, lap.

Assessment: The students will show, with 95% accuracy the highest pitch by placing their hands on their heads.

3. Bernie Bee—Singing Game

Grade Level: First Grade
Music TEKS: Foundations: Creative Expression. The student describes and analyzes musical sound; sing a well-known children's song.
Specific Objective: To teach a song with two tones by rote.
Materials: Bernie Bee, bell set retrieving starting pitch.
Process:
Formation: a seated circle.
Teacher creates a setting for the song: *working in the garden, running away from a bee. Class names types of bees [honey, killer, bumble]. T. could pass around a toy stuffed bee and ask the students to give one word to describe the bee.*

- Students follow teacher and keep a steady beat on their laps and listen for "How many different tones/pitches does the song have?" (2)
- T. sings Bernie Bee and when finished asks "How many different tones . . . ."
- T. points to self and sings first phrase.
- T. points to head for S. to audiate (to sing internally not aloud).
- S. sing phrase aloud.
- T. sings the remaining phrase with S. audiating before singing aloud.
- Students show the two tones by placing the highest one on their head, the middle one on their shoulders. Students follow along with the teacher.
- S. sings without the teacher's help.

Assessment: Aural. Could the students sing Bernie Bee with at least 90% accuracy as a group?
Lesson Extension #1: The game.
Game formation: Circle sitting with '"it" on the outside. Children in the circle sing while "it" walks around the outside of the circle with a bee puppet. At the end of the song "it" drops the bee puppet and runs around the outside of the circle buzzing while the children imitate the buzzing via patching (slapping/patting thighs). On "fly away" the bee puppet is dropped behind a student who picks up the bee and the chase begins while the bass xylophone starts a glissando. You could add more instruments and create a level glissando from low to high range instruments.

Note: Have the two students sitting next to the hole created by the new "it," point to the hole to help the chased student find his resting place. The arrangement below can be played without mallets—using index fingers—to practice a rebound sound. If the student keeps his/her fingers on the bar and not rebound they will not get a tone but a thud. Caution: make sure the students are playing the beat and not the rhythm of the lyrics. If this happens get behind them and gently tap the pattern on their shoulders till they join in on the beat.

Extension #2: Pass the bee around the circle and have each person add on to a story about Bernie Bee that you start.

4.   Mary Ann—Traditional

Grade Level: 3rd Grade
TEKS: Creative expression. The student performs a varied repertoire of developmentally appropriate music in informal or formal settings.

The student is expected to:

3 B. sing or play a varied repertoire of music such as American folk songs and folk songs representative of local cultures independently or in groups;
Specific Objective: The student will sing "Mary Ann" tunefully by memory.
Materials: Mary Ann, melody bells for retrieving starting pitch.
Process:

- "Hi class!" "How would you like to go to the beach today? Does this sound like a good field trip?
- "When was the last time you were at a beach? Name the beach and some activities you would do at a beach."
- S. keep a beat on the floor while teacher sings song and students listen for the girl's name.
- T. asks students the girl's name. Clap the name.
- Teacher sings again by phrase and students to audiate then sing each phrase aloud.
- T. divides class in half. Each half takes turns singing each half of the song Mary Ann.
- S. fill in the blank.
- Sing independently.
- Sing and clap the syncopated rhythm on Mary Ann.

Assessment: Mastery 98–100% of students will sing identify the syncopated rhythm "Mary Ann" by playing it on the hand drum, singing on pitch and independently.

5.   The Noble Duke of York—Traditional Singing Game

Grade Level: 2nd
TEKS: Creative expression. The student performs a varied repertoire of developmentally appropriate music in informal or formal settings. The student is expected to:
A. sing tunefully or play classroom instruments, including rhythmic and melodic patterns, independently or in groups;
B. sing songs or play classroom instruments from diverse cultures and styles, independently or in groups.
Specific Objective: The student will sing, independently and on pitch, *The Noble Duke of York*.
Materials: *The Noble Duke of York*; bell set for retrieving starting pitch.

Process:
Greeting: "Hi friends! How are you doing today?"
Introduction or "hook": "If I were a queen, how would greet me?" Solicit responses.

- S. will keep a beat on their laps as they listen for: the blank or empty spaces in the song.
- T. gives starting pitch to self from bell set then sings song while S. keep a light beat.
- Ask them . . ." Did you hear the empty spaces in the song? I'll sing it again and listen for the word/s before the empty spaces."T. sings while S. keep a quiet beat and listen for the word/s before the empty spaces.
- S. gives T. answers to questions.
- T. points to self and sings first phrase—
- T. points to head for S. to audiate.
- S. sings first phrase aloud.
- T. sings second phrase
- T. points to head for S.to audiate.
- S. sings the second phrase aloud.
- T. adds two phrases together. T. points to self.
- S. audiate, then sing aloud.
- Class sharing by phrase. Split the class in half.
- One half of the class sings the first half of the song.
- The other half now sings the second half of the song.
- Now switch and let the second half start the song.
- S. fills in the blank.
- S. sings by themselves.

Assessment: Intermediate 90–97% of students will be able to sing, independently and on the pitch, the English folk song, *The Noble Duke of York.* Evaluation: By listening/aural, by seeing/visual, I can see and hear if the S. has obtained the objective of singing independently and on pitch, *The Noble Duke of York.*

Extension: On another day students can learn the dance which is connected to the phrases/sentences.
Formation: Longways set facing partner.

- March toward partner (three steps and clap partner's hands on beat 4)
- March backward into original place (three steps backwards and a stomp on beat 4).
- First couple joins both hands and sashsays down and up the longways set.
- First couple casts off with each line following their leader, make an arch at the bottom, lines follow through.
- Game repeats.

Oh the, Noble Duke of York, he had ten thousand men.
He marched them up to the top of the hill and he marched them back again.
And when you're up you're up and when you're down you're down.
And when you're only half way up, you're neither up nor down.
A hunting we will go, a hunting we will go.
We'll catch a fox and put him in a box and then we'll let them go.
A hunting we will go, a hunting we will go.
We'll catch a fox and put him in a box and then we'll let them go.

ENGAGING THE RECORDER

CHAPTER 9

Chapter Objectives

In this chapter, you will be working on two levels of recorder playing. The first will be improving your personal playing ability and the second is recorder pedagogy for children. After completing this chapter, you will be able to:

- apply your musical knowledge to read standard notation and play tunes and songs on the recorder
- learn Soprano Recorder fingerings from low C to high D
- have a foundation for using it as an aid to supplement learning in your classroom

Tooooot! Toooot! Tooooooooooooot! Beautiful music, right? Well, it can be with a lesson plan tailored to your needs. First, you need to decide the purpose of teaching recorder to your students. Are you using the recorder to reinforce singing and reading skills; teach instrumental ensemble playing; or because it's the cheapest individual "classroom" instrument?

Whatever brand of recorder you choose to purchase, a thumb rest, whether a standard part of the recorder, the detachable kind or a homemade one from a bent paperclip with tape, is essential to achieving the proper hand position needed for executing a smooth technique. The thumb rest should be able to hold the weight of the right hand when playing notes requiring the use of only the left hand.

Once you as the teacher feel comfortable playing the soprano recorder, you are ready to execute the plan below for teaching your students this historical instrument. Students like to hear other students. Provide opportunities for student performances. Whatever your initial purpose, your next step is to know and to be able to demonstrate to your students the final product or outcome. Students need to hear (live is best) what they are aiming for in sound production. The students need to produce a clear straight tone with proper articulation (tongue touching on the gum ridge close to the front teeth, but not on them). Proper tone production comes with knowing how much air to use. There are many good recorder tutorial videos online.

TIP BOX

Students like to hear other students. Provide opportunities for student performances.

HISTORY OF THE RECORDER

The recorder is a woodwind musical instrument from the group known as *internal duct flutes*—flutes with a whistle mouthpiece. It has a thumb-hole for the left (the upper) hand with three other holes for the fingers and four finger holes for the right (the bottom) hand. The recorder comes in a variety of voices and sizes. These instruments can be made of wood or plastic.

This instrument was popular in medieval times through the baroque era, but declined in popularity during the 18th century in favor of orchestral woodwind instruments, such as the flute, oboe, and clarinet. The recorder was revived in the 20th century in the pursuit of historically informed performances of early music, and because of its suitability as a simple instrument for teaching music to children.

Image © Mr. Tobin/Shutterstock.com

Skill Development

PRERECORDER EXERCISES

1. Finger presses to recorder music—to coordinate fingers for better success in playing the recorder. Use recordings of solo recorder at first then recordings of recorders in consort. Either press individual fingers onto a desk or finger against finger (making a circle with thumb and index finger, etc.). This stage is important and can be done months ahead of actual recorder instruction. Caution: let the fingers work independently. Do not strain a muscle by using another hand to "help" the fingers.

- Work with one hand.
- Work with the other hand.
- Work both hands together.

2. Air Blowing

Shoulders down, so the lungs will not be stretched vertically and more air can be taken in. Stretch an empty balloon to make the point that you want to keep the shoulders down so you can fill the balloon out. Now blow into the balloon to show how you want the lungs to "look."

Let the mouth open to inhale. You will not have to violently suck in the air. Let the reflexes work. If dizziness occurs, sit down and continue the exercises if you feel like doing so.

3. Tonguing

- Use a "doo" syllable to start the sound, with the tongue tapping the gum ridge behind the top front teeth. Be sure to close the sound at the end of a phrase with a light tap of the tongue back at the starting point; more like a German "du"—the tongue is back.
- Use familiar rhymes for tonguing practice—air tonguing.
- To visualize the concept of *an air stream*, use a string or piece of yarn 3 ft. long. A button which is used to signify the tonguing aspects of the rhythm (of a rhyme) without breathing between each word.
- Lips are lightly closed when tonguing.
- Try the string exercise in groups of three students. One student at each end of the string, holding the string tightly; while the third student moves the button with their hand while air blowing/tonguing a rhyme or song using its rhythm. The object is to "see" the air stream and to see the tonguing of the rhyme or song.
- Vary the rhymes and change position in the exercise.

4. Now for the real McCoy

- Teacher plays a short familiar tune for the students.
- Names are given to the parts of the recorder: head joint, body, foot joint.
- Students take their recorder apart.
- Place tip of mouthpiece in mouth. Cover lips over the mouthpiece and tongue (reminder: tongue touches the ridge of gum behind the front teeth of the mouth) and blow gently. You, as the teacher will need to model often and reteach/remind the students to "blow gently". Let the students experiment. Establish a signal for stopping.
- Echo rhythm patterns from teacher, then from other students.

Note: Concentrate on one sense at a time. Do not add visuals yet (flashcards, notation, etc.).

- Review known rhymes then transfer to the mouthpiece. Break up the rhyme and have individuals take turns playing a phrase. Check for correct tonguing technique. Watch out for "woo woooers" (air puffing, not using their tongue).
- Put the recorder together.
- Affix the thumb rest. This is extremely important for achieving the proper hand position needed for executing a smooth technique. The thumb rest

TIP BOX

When the students enter the room on the day they will put their recorder together, put a sticker (a colored dot will do) on the index finger of the left hand, put a matching dot next to the hole that the finger will cover. Some years, for particular classes I have pre-placed a thin strip of colored tape around the body of the recorder to indicate the separation of the two hands.

Back of Recorder

Image © Cora Bigwood

should be able to hold the weight of the right hand when playing notes requiring the use of only the left hand. The thumb rest is placed behind the 3rd finger (middle finger). A snap on thumb rest can be purchased or you can form one from a plastic covered paper clip and taped on the back of the recorder.

- Which hand on top? Review historical background on hand position. Compare with present day thoughts on the subject of hand position. The answer is: LEFT.

EXPLORATION OF SOUND

1. **Review hand position, tonguing, and air blowing tips.**

    - BAG echo combinations lead by teacher then by students.

2. **Follow the leader game.**

Objective: To strengthen endurance.
Process:

- Teacher chooses a note (B, A, or G) and draws a beat line. The students hold the note the length of the mark on the board. Remind students to start the note with their tongue.
- Students take turns being the leader: choosing the note and lengths of beat lines.

Assessment:
Students analyze their performance in the game. Did they tongue/articulate the start of each tone? Was force/strength/length of air stream appropriate? Did they follow the leader? Stop when leader stopped? Ask the students to tell you how they are stopping the tone.

3. **Student Compositions**

Objective: To create a melodic phrase via speech. (This exercise leads to question and answer experiences.)
Materials: Board, marker, paper, pencils, recorders
Process:

- Teacher writes the following sentence on the board and asks the students to fill in the blanks i.e. Mad Libs.

I like to (verb) my (noun/thing) to (noun/place) every (day of the week).

- Students recite sentence. Teacher circles sentence fragments.

I like to (verb) my (noun/thing) to (noun/place) every (day of the week).

- Students assign a pitch to each circle—pitches can repeat:

I like to walk my dog to the park every Wednesday.

Example: B   B   A   G

- Play the above example on the recorder. You can also sing the example and add a simple accompaniment on a xylophone or bell set by playing a G and D on the beats.
- Students find a partner. Hand out paper and pencil to each group.
- Students create a sentence using the same format above or they can create one of their own length and subject matter.

Assessment:
Did the students follow instructions?
Did the student play with finesse: using proper air force, tonguing, and closure of last note? Some of the time? All of the time? Not at all.

4. **Questions and Answers**

Objective: To improvise melodic phrases using BAG.
Materials: Soprano recorder, board, markers.
Process:

- Ask the students (individually) some simple questions, i.e., Did you have a lot of homework last night? Yes and I didn't get it all done.

What will you do this weekend? I'm going to the movies and out for a pizza.

- Display a question and an answer on the board.
- Circle sections and assign pitches. For the question start with G and end on B. For the Answer start on B and end on G.
- Sing Q & A using solfege (mrd) and hand signs. Transfer to pitch names (singing), fingering the notes on the recorder. Play melody on the recorder.

5. **Extension of Question and Answer Activity**

Objective: To have the students become comfortable with creating short melodic phrases within a framework.
Materials: Soprano recorders
Process:

- Play a short melody using BAG, a musical question and ask the students to respond as a group—(their answers will be different).
- Now choose individuals for a response with you. Have them start with the pitch that you ended with and to end on the tonic/home pitch (the one you started with). Discuss length of each Q & A. Beat lines could be drawn on the board for reference.
- Have the students choose a partner for individual question and response practice. Give a sound cue on the drum or other instrument as a cue for students to switch roles.
- Ask for volunteers to share their Q & A with the class. Discuss how each group decided upon the length of their Q & A.

TIP BOX

When playing patterns for the students to repeat, always start with a small range and move that range from stepwise to small skips.
Always use a clear tone with no vibrato—for intonation and style reasons.

- Choose pairs of students to perform their Q & A during the improvisation section of the rondo.
- Have one student improvise at a time.

Adding Standard Music Notation

6. **Starting with B A G—A Pentatonic Sequence**

Front of the Recorder

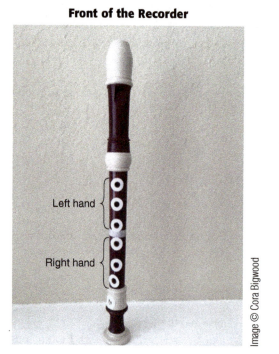

Left hand

Right hand

Image © Cora Bigwood

Fingering for B

Image © Cora Bigwood

Warming Up On B

Fingering for A

Image © Cora Bigwood

The A Game

Fingering for G

G Whiz

Steps and Skips

Hot Cross Buns

Traditional

Hot cross buns,   hot cross buns,   one a pen-ny two a pen-ny   hot cross buns.

Closet Key

Traditional

Bow Wow Wow

You will only play measures 1, 2 and 4 while the teacher sings the song.

Singing Game

Frog in the Millpond

Ridin' in the Buggy

American Folk Song

Merrily We Roll Along

Traditional

(musical notation)

Mer - ri - ly we roll a - long, roll a - long, roll a - long. Mer - ri - ly we

(musical notation)

roll   a - long,   on   the   deep   blue   sea.

Hop Old Squirrel

Traditional

(musical notation)

Hop old squirrel,   Ei - dle dum, ei - dle dum. Hop old squirrel,   ei - dle-dum dee.

(musical notation)

Hop   old squirrel,   ei - dle dum,   ei - dle dum,   hop   old squirrel,   ei - dle dum dee.

Verses: 2. Jump old squirrel . . . 3. Run old squirrel . . . 4. Hide old squirrel . . .
Game. One student is the "squirrel" who acts out the lyrics we sing. On last word, student freezes behind someone, that person becomes the next "squirrel". On "hide," students sitting in the circle close eyes . . .

Long-Legged Sailor

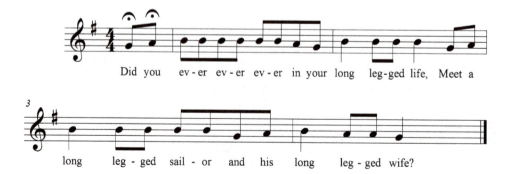

Did you   ev - er ev - er ev - er in your long   leg-ged life, Meet a

long   leg - ged sail - or   and his   long   leg - ged wife?

Alice the Camel

Al-ice, the ca-mel has   (x) humps,   Al-ice, the ca-mel has   (x) humps,

Al - ice,   the ca-mel has   (x) humps so   go,   Al - ice,   go!

Game: Children stand in a circle with their arms linked. Every time you sing a number (on the x) you bob up and down one time. At the end of each verse sway hips from side to side, gently bumping the person next to you while saying the word, "Boom" for the number of humps in that verse. Example—3 humps would be, "Boom, boom, boom." Count down to 0 and at the end of that verse say, "So Alice is a HORSE—of course!"

7.   **Using the same echo process and move on to low E and low D.**

E Is For Exercise

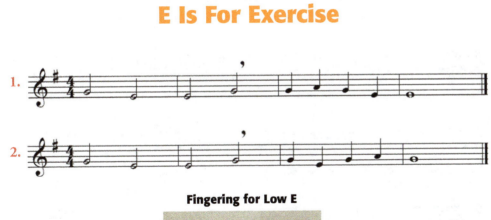

1.

2.

Fingering for Low E

Image © Cora Bigwood

Yangtze

Chinese Folk Tune

Step Back Baby

New York Children's Singing Game

Not last night but the night be - fore, step back ba - by step back.

Twen-ty-four rob-bers at my door. Step back bab-y step back. O-pened up the door and I let them in.

Step back ba - by step back. Hit 'em on the head with a rol-ling pin. Step back ba - by step back.

Should have seen the way that the rob - bers ran. Step back bab - y step back.

Some ran east and some ran west. Step back bab - y step back. Step back bab - y step back.

Skin and Bones

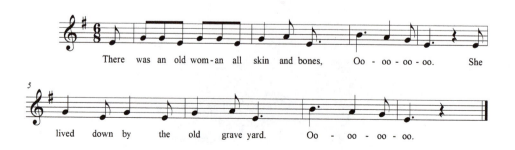

There was an old wom-an all skin and bones, Oo - oo - oo - oo. She

lived down by the old grave yard. Oo - oo - oo - oo.

Verses:

2. One night she thought she'd take a walk, Oo.... She walked down by the old grave yard, Oo...
3. She saw the bones a-layin' around, Oo... She thought she'd sweep the old graveyard, Oo...
4. She went to the closet to get a broom, Oo.... She opened the door and BOO!

We Are Playing in the Forest

Traditional Melody

Mongolian Night Song

Traditional Mongolian Song

Verse 2: In the moonlight's golden glow, Soft the wind begins to blow.
Little lambs are fast asleep, lying by the other sheep. Still a silent watch she keeps.
All alone she waits. "When I'm tending all alone, all I think about is home."

Fingering for D

Image © Cora Bigwood

D Is For Disco

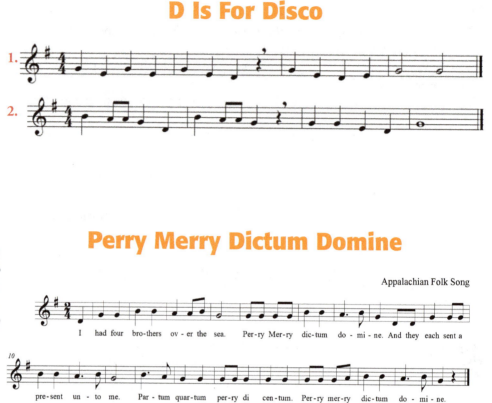

Perry Merry Dictum Domine

Appalachian Folk Song

I had four bro-thers ov-er the sea. Per-ry Mer-ry dic-tum do - mi - ne. And they each sent a

pre-sent un - to me. Par - tum quar-tum per-ry di cen-tum. Per-ry mer-ry dic-tum do - mi - ne.

Verses:
The first sent a chicken without any bone
The second a cherry without any stone.

The third sent a book that no man could read
The fourth sent a blanket without any thread.

How could there be a chicken without any bone?
How could there be a cherry without any stone?

How could there be a book that no man could read?
How could there be a blanket without any thread?

When the chicken is in the egg, it has no bone
When the cherry is in the blossom it has no stone.

When the book is in the press, no man can it read
When the blanket is in the fleece it has no thread.

Jolly Old Saint Nicholas

My Horses Ain't Hungry

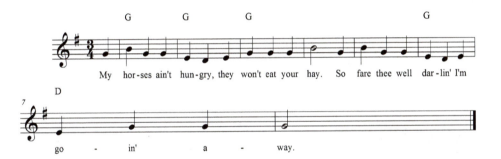

Old Brass Wagon

Verses: 2. Circle to the right . . . 3. Ev'rybody in. . . . 4. Ev'rybody out . . .

8. Now Take Note!

Objective: To identify a known melody through standard notation.
Materials: Long-Legged Sailor (or another song with which they are familiar)
Process:

1. Hand out Long-Legged Sailor without the title. Ask the students to look at the melodic line—the direction of the melody.
2. Clap out rhythms. Can you name that tune?
3. Give the students a minute to work on playing it from the notation.

Assessment:

- Did the student meet the objective? Novice: 80–89%
- Did the student exceed the objective? Intermediate: 90–97%
- Did the student master the objective? Mastery: 98–100%

9.   Add the F#

F# Exercise

Fingering for F#

Image © Cora Bigwood

Au Claire De La Lune

French Folk Song

Stand ing in the moon light, Mon a - mi Pier - rot.   I have lost my

can - dle, how I do not know!   If you can not help me,   I will have to

stay.   Stand ing in the dark ness,   'til the light of day.

Sally Go 'Round the Sun

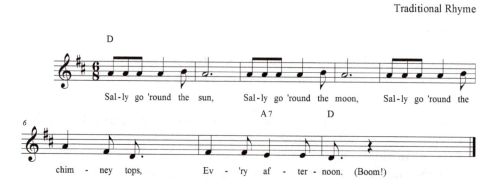

Traditional Rhyme

Sal - ly go 'round the sun,   Sal - ly go 'round the moon,   Sal - ly go 'round the

chim - ney tops,   Ev - 'ry af - ter - noon. (Boom!)

10. Add High C'

Sail On the High C

Fingering for High C

Image © Cora Bigwood

Flowers

French Folk Tune

Yankee Doodle

You will only be able to play the verse of Yankee Doodle on your recorder. The refrain has notes that are out of the Soprano Recorder range.

Traditional Melody

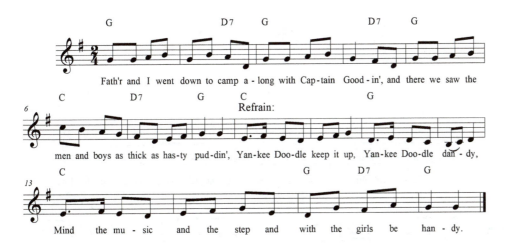

Fath'r and I went down to camp a-long with Cap-tain Good-in', and there we saw the
men and boys as thick as has-ty pud-din', Yan-kee Doo-dle keep it up, Yan-kee Doo-dle dan-dy,
Mind the mu-sic and the step and with the girls be han-dy.

Verses:

2. Yankee Doodle went to town, a riding on a pony, He stuck a feather in his cap and called it macaroni. Refrain.

3. There was Captain Washington upon a slapping stallion, a-giving orders to his men; I guess there were a million.

Fingering for High D

Image © Cora Bigwood

11. Add High D'

Dive From the High D

Mary Had A Little Lamb

Chatter With the Angels

Who's Got A Fishpole

American Folk Song

Who's got a fish - pole? We do! Who's got a fish - pole? We do!

Who's got a fish - pole? We do! Fish - pole needs a line.

12. Adding Both High C' and High D'

El charro

Mexican Folk Song

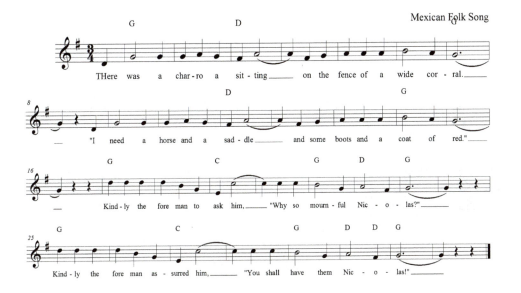

THere was a char-ro a sit-ting_____ on the fence of a wide cor-ral._____

___ "I need a horse and a sad-dle_____ and some boots and a coat of red."_____

___ Kind-ly the fore man to ask him,_____ "Why so mourn-ful Nic-o-las?"_____

Kind-ly the fore man as-surred him,_____ "You shall have them Nic-o-las!"_____

Verse 2.
"Just one more thing," said el charro, "I would marry your daughter, too,"
Firmly the foreman assured him, "She is taken, Nicolás."
Charro cried out, despairing, "I will throw myself off a cliff!"
Kindly the foreman suggested, "Then go head first, Nicolás!"

Lightly Row

Traditional

Aunt Rhody

Traditional

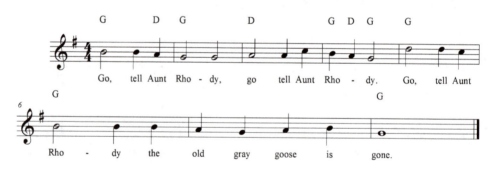

Jingle Bells

James Pierpont

Ode to Joy

Beethoven

13. **For those who would like to continue and play a fuller range of the Soprano Recorder, let's add**

Bb, F; and middle C.

Fingering for Bb

B Flat Tire

Image © Cora Bigwood

Fingering for F

Image © Cora Bigwood

Exercise For F(un)

Fingering for Low C

Image © Cora Bigwood

Low C Workout

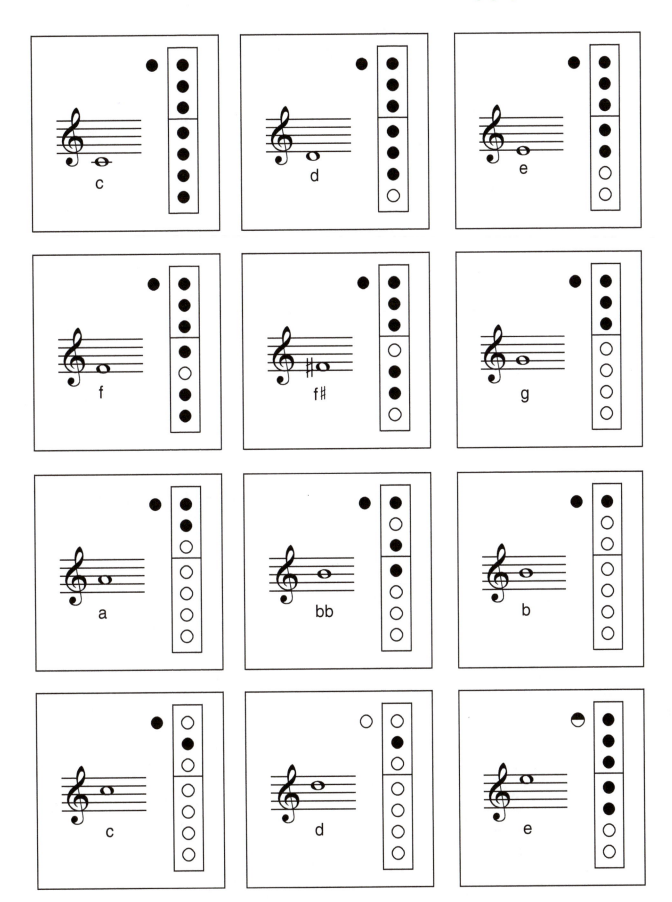

MUSIC LIBRARY

SONG LIST IN ALPHABETICAL ORDER

A Hunting We Will Go

English Singing Game

Oh a hunt-ing we will go. A hunt-ing we will go. We'll catch a fox and put him in a box and then we'll let him go.

America

Words by Rev. Samuel Francis Smith

My coun-try 'tis of thee sweet land of li - ber-ty of thee I sing: land where my fa - ther's died land of the pil - grim's pride from ev - ery mountain side let free - dom ring!

America, The Beautiful

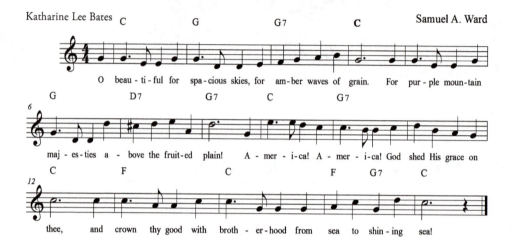

2. O beautiful for Pilgrim feet, whose stern impassioned stress. A thoroughfare for freedom beat across the wilderness.

    America! America! God mend thine every flaw, confirm thy soul in self-control, thy liberty in law.

3. O beautiful for heroes proved in liberating strife. Who more than self their country loved, and mercy more than life.

    America! America! May God thy gold refine till all success be nobleness and every gain divine.

4. O beautiful for patriot dream that sees beyond the years. Thine alabaster cities gleam undimmed by human tears.

    America! America! God shed His grace on thee, and crown thy good with brotherhood from sea to shining sea.

Apple Tree

Game Directions: Form a circle. Begin with the teacher and another student forming a tree (bridge) for students to walk under as they sing the song, keeping the beat with their feet. On the final word "out," the branches come down over a student. That student becomes the next helper and the original student walks in a circle to continue the game.

Extension: After learning the game, each time another student is caught under the branches, new trees are formed until all students are trees. The teacher helps when there is an odd number.

A Ram Sam Sam

Folk Song from Morocco

A ram sam sam, a ram sam sam, gu-li gu-li gu-li gu-li gu-li ram sam sam. A

ra - fi, a ra - fi, gu-li gu-li gu-li gu-li gu-li ram sam sam.

A Sailor Went to Sea

Traditional

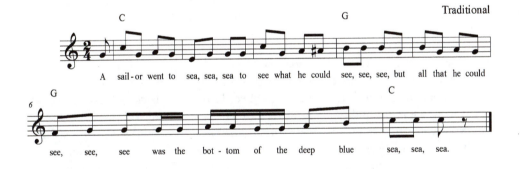

A sail-or went to sea, sea, sea to see what he could see, see, see, but all that he could

see, see, see was the bot-tom of the deep blue sea, sea, sea.

2. chop, chop, chop
3. knee, knee, knee
4. tap, tap, tap
5. oo watchee-wa

Bernie Bee

American Singing Game

Ber - nie Bee, Ber - nie Bee, tell me when your wed-ding be.

If it be to-mor-row day take your wings and fly a - way.

Bill Grogan's Goat

Folk Song

2. One day the goat (one day the goat) Felt frisk and fine: (felt frisk and fine:)
   Ate three red shirts (ate three red shirts) Right off the line. (right off the line).
   The man, he grabbed (the man, he grabbed) Him by the back, (him by the back)
   And tied him to (and tied him to (A railroad track.) A railroad track.

3. Now, when that train (now when that train) Hove into sight, (hove into sight)
   That goat grew pale (that goat grew pale) And green with fright, (and green
   with fright) He heaved a sigh, (he heaved a sigh) As if in pain; (as if in pain)
   Coughed up the shirts (coughed up the shirts) And flagged the train.(And
   flagged the train)

Bounce High, Bounce Low

Traditional

Bow Wow Wow

Singing Game

Bow, wow, wow.   Whose dog art thou?   Lit-tle Tom-my Tuck-er's dog bow, wow, wow.

Formation: Circle, standing.

Finding a starting point, two people face each other. Continue pattern.

Measure 1: Step feet on "Bow wow wow".

Measure 2: Stretch hands out to each side.

Measure 3: Holding both hands of partner, change places.

Measure 4: Step feel on "Bow wow wow". Jump/turn around.

Repeat song with new partner.

Extension: Class can create an introduction using names of dog breeds said in a rhythmic pattern. Example: Ger-man shep-herd. Rott - wei-ler, pug (quarter rest), bull dog.

Buffalo Gals

American Folk Song

As I was lum-bring down the street, - down the street, - down the street, - a pret-ty lit-tle gal I chanched to meet, - Oh she was fair to view. Buf-fa-lo gals, won't ya come out to-night, come out to-night, come out to-night. Buf-fa-lo gals, won't ya come out to - night, and dance by the light of the moon.

2. I asked her if she'd have a talk, have a talk, have a talk. Her feet took up the whole sidewalk as she stood close to me. (Refrain)

3. I asked her "Would you want to dance, want to dance, want to dance?" I thought that I would have a chance to shake a foot with her.(Refrain)

4. Oh, I danced with the gal with a hole in her stockin', and her hip kept a-rockin', and her toe kept a-knockin'. I danced with the gal with the hole in her stockin' and we danced by the light of the moon. (Refrain)

5. I wanna make that gal my wife, gal my wife, gal my wife. Then I'd be happy all my life if I had her with me.(Refrain)

Camptown Races

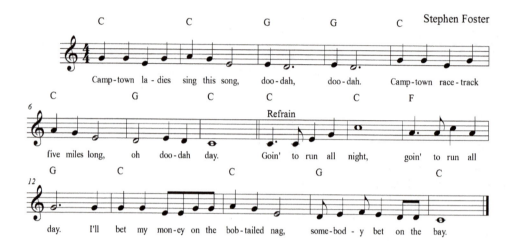

2. Oh, the long tailed filly and the big black horse, doo-dah, doo dah.
   Come to a mud hole and they all cut across, oh doo-dah day. (Refrain)
3. I went down there with my hat caved in, doo-dah, doo-dah. I came back home
   with a pocket full of tin, oh doo-dah day. (Refrain)

Charlie Over the Ocean

Game directions:

1. Teach the echo song.
2. Game objective is for the "it" to choose a person to chase him/her.
3. Formation is a seated circle with the "it" walking counter clockwise around the
   outside of the circle.
4. The "it" starts the echo song.

Chicken on a Fence Post

American Singing Game

Game directions:

1. Teach the song by Rote method.
2. Game objective is for the "farmers" to race and get the chicken from inside the circle.
3. Choose two "farmers" who hide their eyes
4. Place a rubber chicken inside the circle.
5. Designate two students to be the "gate".
6. Begin singing the song, students join hands and move counter clockwise. "Farmers are walking around the outside of the circle."
7. At the end of the song, the gate opens and the "farmers" race to grab the chicken first (and have dinner that evening!).

Cindy

American Folk Song

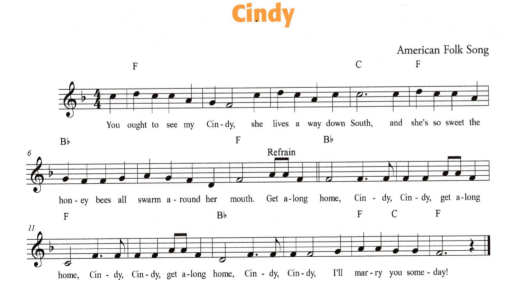

2. She loves me in the summertime, she loves me in the fall. If she don't love me all the time I want no love at all. (Refrain)
3. I wish I were an apple a-hanging on the tree and every time that Cindy passed she'd take a bite of me. (Refrain)

Circle 'Round the Zero

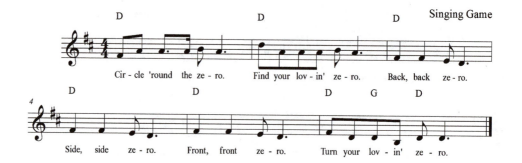

Clementine

De Colores

Folk song from Mexico

When ___ the mead - ows, ___ when the mead - ows burst forth in the cool, dew - y
col - ors of spring - time; ___ When ___ the swal - lows, ___
___ when the swal - lows come wing - ing in clouds of bright col - ors from far off; ___
___ When ___ the rain - bow, ___ when the rain - bow spreads rib - bons of col - or all
o - ver the sky; ___ then I know why the splen - dors of true love are great and their
col - ors the best ones of all. ___ Then I best ones of all. ___

Down by the Station

American Folk Song

Down by the sta - tion ear - ly in the morn - ing, see the lit - tle puf - fer bel - lies all in a row.

See the en - gine dri - ver pull the lit - tle han - dle, chug, chug, toot, toot, off they go.

Down in the Valley

2. Hear the wind blow, love, hear the wind blow.
   Hang your head over, hear the wind blow.
3. If you don't love me, love whom you please.
   Throw your arms round me, give my heart ease.
4. Give my heart ease, love, give my heart ease.
   Throw your arms round me, give my heart ease.
5. Write me a letter, send it by mail.
   Send it in care of Birmingham Jail.
6. Birmingham Jail, love, Birmingham Jail.
   Send it in care of Birmingham Jail.
7. Writing this letter, containing three lines.
   Answer my question, "Will you be mine?"
8. Will you be mine, dear, will you be mine?
   Answer my question, "Will you be mine?"
9. Build me a castle forty feet high.
   So I can see her as she goes by.
10. As she goes by, dear, as she goes by.
    So I can see her as she goes by.
11. Roses love sunshine, violets love dew.
    Angels in Heaven know I love you.

Do Your Ears Hang Low?

2. Do your ears flip flop? Can you use them for a mop? Are they stringy at the bottom? Are they curly at the top? Can you use them for a swatter? Can you use them for a blotter? Do your ears flip flop?

3. Do your ears hang wide? Do they flap from side to side? Do they wave in the breeze? From the slightest little sneeze? Can you soar above the nation with a feeling of elation? Do your ears hang wide?

Draw Me a Bucket of Water

American Play Party

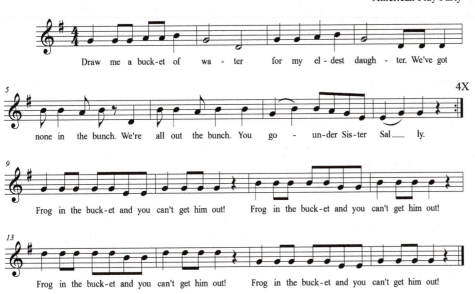

El Floron

Puerto Rican Singing Game

Erie Canal

Work Song

Found a Peanut

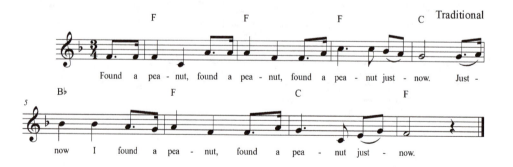

2. Cracked it open . . .
3. It was rotten . . .
4. Ate it anyway . . .
5. Got a stomach ache . . .

6. Called the doctor . . .
7. Penicillin . . .
8. Operation . . .
9. Died anyway . . .
10. Went to Heaven . . .
11. Wouldn't take me . . .
12. Went the other way . . .
13. Didn't want me . . .
14. Was a dream . . .
15. Then I woke up . . .
16. Found a peanut . . .

Frog Went A Courtin'

Library of Congress AFS 656A
Collected by John A. Lomax

2. He rode up to Miss Mousie's door, m-hm, m-hm. He rode up to Miss Mousie's door and where he'd often been before, m-hm, m-hm.

3. He took Miss Mousie on his knee, m-hm, m-hm. He took Miss Mousie on his knee, and said, Miss Mousie, will you marry me? M-hm, m-hm.

4. I can't answer yes to that, m-hm, m-hm. I can't answer yes to that, till I see my Uncle Rat m-hm, m-hm.

Grand Old Flag

George M. Cohan

Grizzly Bear

Erling Bisgaard and Gulie Stehouwer

1. Teach the song by rote, starting song very quietly and getting louder as the Bear is awakened.
2. Discuss science information about a Bear and hibernation.
3. Seat children in rows facing one child at the front who is the "Bear".
4. The Bear hides his/her eyes while children sing.
5. Teacher points at one child to come up silently and tap the Bear and run back to place.
6. As children increase volume, the Bear jumps up and growls. The Bear gets three guesses as to who was the tapper.
7. The tapper becomes the Bear and the game continues.

TIP BOX

Learning to play a game honestly and fairly is something all children need to learn. As humans, it is so tempting to point or blurt out the answer, so don't be surprised when it happens in small children. The teacher should always have gentle ways to explain about making the game more fun, being a good sport and including everyone in a game. Say these reminders before every game just to head these temptations off at the pass.

Hawaiian Rainbows

Hawaiian Folk Song

Head and Shoulders, Baby

African American Singing Game

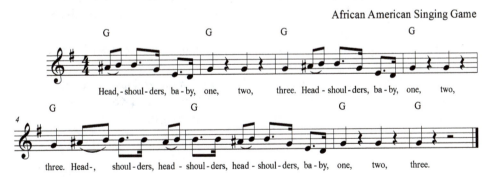

2. Shoulders-chest . . .
3. Chest to knees . . .
4. Knees to ankles . . .
5. Ankles-knees . . .
6. Knees to chest . . .
7. Chest to shoulders . . .
8. Shoulders-head . . .
9. That's all . . .

Game directions:
Facing partner do #1: touch own head and shoulders (this changes with each verse).
Clap own hands; clap partner's right hand; clap own hands; clap partner's left hand; clap own hands; clap both of partner's hands together.

Hello There!

Traditional

Hel - lo there,   (Hel - lo   there)   How   are   you?   (How   are   you?)   It's

so good,   (It's   so   good)   to   see   you,   (to see you)   We'll   sing   and,   (we'll   sing   and)   be

hap - py,   (be hap - py)   We're   all   here   to - ge - ther   a - gain!

This song is a wonderful first day song to greet and meet all the students and to create a relaxed and safe atmosphere in the classroom.

1. Teach the song by rote. Have students join the teacher for the last phrase, circling arms up and around on "We're all here together again".
2. Sing again asking children to add a wave back to the teacher during each phrase.
3. Sing again asking children to add a wave and make eye contact to different people in the room, each phrase.
4. Sing again asking children to randomly walk around the room waving and smiling at each person they pass by.
5. Stop and form groups of 4 students. Share first names and answer an easy question, "What is your favorite color?" or "What is your favorite food to eat?"
6. Sing again, form new groups and answer questions again.

Here Comes a Bluebird

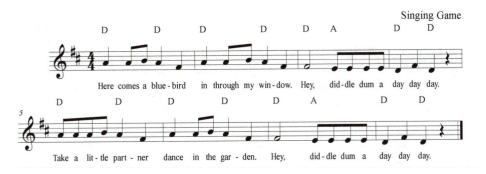

Game directions:
Formation - circle standing with hands joined and held upward. One child walks in and under the arches. On "take a little partner" this child takes a partner and with two hands joined, face each other and gallop out through the opening and back again or dance around inside of the ring. The first child joins the ring with the partner becoming the bluebird.

Here We Go Looby Loo

He's Got the Whole World

2. He's got the little bitty baby . . .
3. He's got you and me brother . . .
4. He's got everybody here . . .

Hokey-Pokey

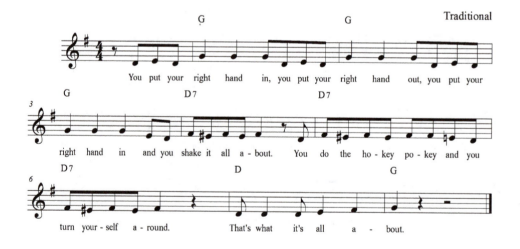

2. You put your left hand in . . .
3. . . . right foot in . . .
4. . . . left foot in . . .
5. . . . right shoulder in . . .
6. . . . left shoulder in . . .
7. . . . right hip in . . .
8. . . . left hip in . . .
9. . . . head in . . .
10. . . . whole self in . . .

Hush Little Baby

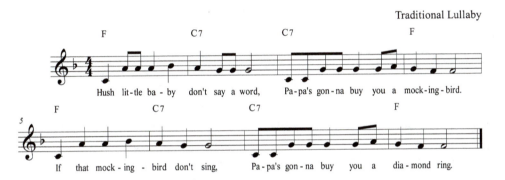

Traditional Lullaby

Hush lit-tle ba - by don't say a word, Pa-pa's gon-na buy you a mock-ing-bird.

If that mock-ing - bird don't sing, Pa-pa's gon-na buy you a dia-mond ring.

2. And if that diamond ring turns brass, Pappa's gonna buy you a looking glass.
3. And if that looking glass gets broke, Papa's gonna buy you a billy goat.
4. And if that billy goat won't pull, Papa's gonna buy you a cart and bull.
5. And if that cart and bull turn over, Papa's gonna buy you a dog named Rover.
6. And if that dog named Rover won't bark, Papa's gonna buy you a horse and cart.
7. And if that horse and cart fall down, you'll still be the sweetest little baby in town.

I Have a Car

Camp Song

I have a car it's made of tin. No-bo-dy knows what shape it's in. It

has four wheels and a rum-ble seat. Hear us chug-ging down the street. Honk

honk rat-tle rat-tle rat-tle crash beep beep, Honk honk rat-tle rat-tle rat-tle crash beep beep, Honk

honk rat-tle rat-tle rat-tle crash beep beep, Honk honk!

Motions: Pretend to "Drive"
"Honk, honk"—pound fist
"Rattle, rattle"—twist body
"Toot"—pat legs
"Crash"—clap
"Beep, beep"—tap nose

I Love the Mountains

Folk Song

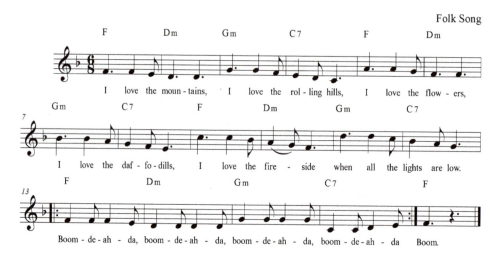

F   Dm   Gm   C7   F   Dm

I love the moun-tains, I love the rol-ling hills, I love the flow-ers,

Gm   C7   F   Dm   Gm   C7

I love the daf-fo-dills, I love the fire-side when all the lights are low.

F   Dm   Gm   C7   F

Boom-de-ah-da, boom-de-ah-da, boom-de-ah-da, boom-de-ah-da Boom.

Game directions:

1. Teach the song by rote.
2. Add simple motions for key words, or use American Sign Language for key words found in an online dictionary.
3. Sing with motions, then sing in a round to create harmony.

Ida Red

Folk Song from Kentucky

I'm a Nut

Camp Song

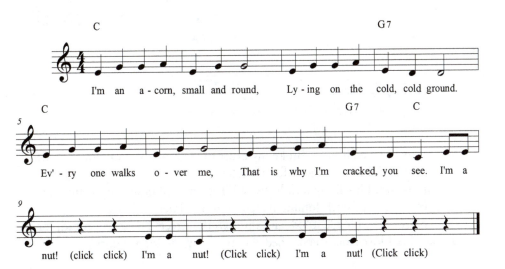

2. Called myself on the telephone, Just to hear my golden tone,
   Asked me out for a little date, Picked me up about half past eight.
   I'm a nut, I'm a nut, I'm a nut.
3. Took myself to the movie show, Stayed too late and said, "Let's go."
   Took my hand and led me out, Drove me home and gave a shout!
   I'm a nut, I'm a nut, I'm a nut.

John Jacob Jingleheimer Schmidt

Camp Song

John Ja-cob Jing-le-heim-er Schmidt, His name is my name too. When-ever I go out, the peo-ple al-ways shout, "There goes John Ja-cob Jing-le-heim-er Schmidt," Da da da da da da da da.

Johnny Has Gone for a Soldier

Traditional Folk Song

Here I sit on But-ter-milk Hill. Who can blame me, cry my fill. And ev'-ry tear would turn a mill. John-ny has gone for a sold-ier.

2. Me, oh my, I loved him so. Broke my heart to see him go. And only time will heal my woe, Johnny has gone for a soldier.

3. I'll sell my rod, I'll sell my reel, likewise I'll sell my spinning wheel, and buy my love a sword of steel, Johnny has gone for a soldier.

4. I'll dye my dress, I'll dye it red, and through the streets I'll beg for bread, for the lad that I love from me has fled, Johnny has gone for a soldier.

John the Rabbit

American Traditional

Oh, John the rab - bit, (oh, yes). Had a migh - ty hab - bit, (oh, yes). Get - tin'
in my gar - den, (oh, yes). Eat - 'in up my cab - bage, (oh, yes). My red to - ma - toes, (oh, yes). My
sweet po - ta - toes, (oh, yes). And if I live - (oh, yes) to see next fall - (oh, yes). I'm
not gon - na have, (oh, yes), an - y gar - den at all. (Oh, yes)!

Note: Students can add other plants that grow in a garden that John could eat.

Juanito (in Spanish)

Children's Song from Spain

Juan - i - to, cuan - do bai - la, bai - la, bai - la, bai - la. Juan - i - to, cuan - do bai - la,
bai - la con la ma - no. Con la ma - no, ma - no, ma - no. Ay que bien bai - la Juan - i - to.

2. Juanito, cuando baila, baila, baila, baila.
   Juanito, cuando baila, baila con el dedito.
   Con el didito, dito, dito. ay que bien baila Juanito!
3. Juanito, cuando baila . . . con el pie . . .
4. Juanito, cuando baila . . . . con la cabeza . . .

Juanito (in English)

1. When Little Johnny dances, dances dances, dances. When Little Johnny dances, dances with his hand - with his hand, hand, hand. Oh, how smartly Johnny dances!
2. When little Johnny dances, dances, dances, dances. When Little Johnny dances, dances with his pinkie. With his pinkie, pinkie, pinkie. Oh, how smartly Johnny dances!
3. When Little Johnny dances, . . . with his foot . . .
4. When Little Johnny dances . . . with his head . . .
5. When Little Johnny dances, . . . with his shoulder . . .
6. When Little Johnny dances, . . . with his elbow . . .

Juba

African American game song

Ju - ba this and   Ju - ba that,   Ju - ba caught a   yel - low cat.

Ju - ba up and   Ju - ba down,   Ju - ba run - ning   all a - round.

Game Directions:

Make space in the room to play the game. There must be room for a large circle with space to run behind the circle.

1. Teach the song by rote.
2. Have students stand in a circle with a little space between them. One student, "Juba" is outside the circle and another student, "Cat" is inside the circle.
3. Children hold hands while singing, moving them up and down on those words. At the end of the song, children drop hands and stand like statues.
4. Juba starts chasing the cat. The cat may go in and out and around the circle as Juba tries to tap the cat. This game is different from "Duck, Duck, Goose" in that Juba does not have to follow the step of the cat but may cut off angles, going across the circle, in and out, any direction. This requires more thinking ahead and planning how to tag the cat. (Geometry cross curricular link).
5. Juba wins by tagging the cat, but the cat wins when teacher calls "time up" for the chase.
6. Juba and Cat pick another child to replace them and the game begins again.

Jump Jim Joe

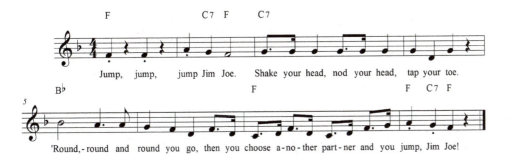

Traditional singing game

Jump, jump, jump Jim Joe. Shake your head, nod your head, tap your toe.

'Round, - round and round you go, then you choose a-no-ther part-ner and you jump, Jim Joe!

Game Directions:

This singing game is perfect for fun and including all children. It can be used with large groups.

Rule #1: To be inclusive, respectful and fair, once the game starts you must play the game if someone chooses you to be their partner.

Tip for the students: This game moves so fast, you don't have time to look for your best pal to be your partner. Just find a living, breathing human and keep going!

Rule #2: You can't choose a partner who is standing until everyone who is seated has been chosen.

Tip #2 If you can't find a partner easily, hold your hand straight up in the air and look across the crowd for someone else with their hand up. Run to them and play!

1. Teach the song by rote.
2. Teach the motions. Partners hold hands and jump, shake and nod head, tap right toe, do a "wring the dishrag" movement (both pair of hands move up to the right and over head, turning the whole body, without letting go of the partner's hands. Make one complete rotation. This can be hard for children to do, so practice this move separately). Partners let go of hands on the final phrase and will turn quickly to find another partner.
3. Sit children in a circle. Choose one person to start the game. He/She stands in front of another child who is seated.
4. The seated child stands up, joins hands with the partner and all begin to sing the song.
5. Each child chooses another partner and now there are two sets playing the game. Next time 4 sets are participating and on and on.
6. Keep singing the song and choosing new partners until everyone who is seated is in the game.
7. Now all are standing, singing and choosing new partners. Fun!
8. Keep singing the song with no break. This keeps everyone moving quickly. Keep singing and finding new partners until the teacher stops the game.

Cross curricular with Math—Have children count by doubling numbers to see how many children will eventually be in the game if you start with the first two. 2, 4, 8, 16, 32, etc.

Ask, How many time will we sing the game before everyone is up and playing?

Kaeru no Uta (Frog's Song)

Japanese Folk Song

Kookaburra

Australian Folk Song

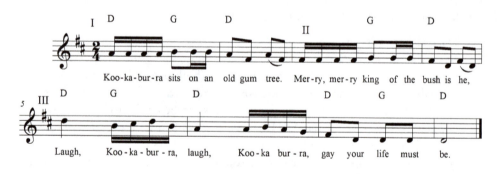

Lil' Liza Jane

Traditional

2. I got a house in Baltimore, Li'l Liza Jane,
   Brussels carpet on the floor, Li'l Liza Jane. Refrain
3. I got a house in Baltimore, Li'l Liza Jane, Silver doorplate on the door,
   Li'l Liza Jane. Refrain
4. Come, my love and be with me, Li'l Liza Jane, And I'll take good care of thee,
   Li'l Liza Jane. Refrain

Little Johnny Brown

African American Singing Game

From *LITTLE JOHN BROWN*. New words and new music adaptation by Bessie Jones. Collected and edited with new material by Alan Lomax. TRO-© Copyright 1972 (Renewed) Ludlow Music, Inc., New York, NY. International Copyright Secured. Made in U.S.A. All Rights Reserved Including Public Performance For Profit. Used by Permission.

In the repeated measures, sing while you follow the directions in the music:

2. Give it to another, Johnny Brown,
   Give it to another, Johnny Brown.
3. Make a little motion, Johnny Brown,
   Make a little motion, Johnny Brown.

Little Sally Walker

Southern African American Ring Game

Lit-tle Sal-ly Wal-ker sit-ting in a sauc-er cry-in' out her eyes for all she's done.

Rise Sal-ly rise wipe the tears from your eyes. Put your hands on your hip let your back-bone slip.

Shanke it to the east. Shake it to the west. Shake it to the one that you like the best, Sal-ly.

Long-legged Sailor

Did you ev-er ev-er ev-er in your long leg-ged life, Meet a

long leg-ged sail-or and his long leg-ged wife?

2. No I never, never, never in my long- legged life . . .
3. Have you ever, ever, ever in your short-legged life . . .
4. No I never, never, never in my short-legged life . . .
5. Have you ever, ever, ever in your bow-legged life . . .
6. No I never, never, never in my bow-legged life . . .
7. Have you ever, ever, ever in your knock-kneed life . . .
8. No I never, never, never in my knock kneed life . . .

MOTIONS:

This is a clapping game performed in pairs.
"Have"—Slap own thighs
"you"—clap own hands
"ever"—with partner, clap right hands
"ever"—clap own hands
"ever"—with partner, clap left hands
"in your"—clap own hands
"long"—spread hands wide apart
"legged"—clap own hands

"life"—with partner, clap right hands
"seen a"—clap own hands
"long"—spread hands wide apart
"legged"—clap own hands
"sailor"—with partner, clap left hands
"with a"—clap own hands
"long"—spread hands wide apart
"legged"—clap own hands
"wife"—clap partner's hands.

On Other Verses:

"short"—put hands right next to each other in front of you.
"bow"—put arms over head in a bowed motion or bend legs outward like a "bow legged cowboy."
"Knock kneed"—bend and knock your knees together.

Los pollitos (Little Chickens)

Folk Song from Ecuador

Mary Ann

Mi cuerpo hace musica

Hispanic Folk Song

Miss Mary Mack

African-American Singing Game

2. She asked her mother, mother, mother
   For 50 cents, cents, cents
   To see the elephants, elephants, elephants
   Jump over the fence, fence, fence.

3. They jumped so high, high, high
   They reached the sky, sky, sky
   And they didn't come back, back, back
   'Til the 4th of July, ly, ly!

Mon papa (My Papa)

Folk Song from France

My pa-pa will say no, No more danc-ing, no more danc-ing,

My pa-pa will say no, No more pol-ka danc-ing now!

2. Oh papa, dear papa, Let me go and dance the polka,
   Oh, papa, dear papa, Let me dance the polka now!

Mulberry Bush

Traditional

Here we go 'round the mul-ber-ry bush, the mul-ber-ry bush, the mul-ber-ry bush.

Here we go 'round the mul-ber-ry bush, so ear-ly in the morn-ing.

My Aunt Came Back

Camp Song

My aunt came back, (my aunt came back) from Hol-land too, (from Hol-land too) And she brought with her, (and she brought with her) a wood-en shoe, (a wood-en shoe)

Verses:

2.   My aunt came back from old Japan, and she brought with her a waving fan.
3.   My aunt came back from old Tangiers, and she brought with her a pair of shears.
4.   My aunt came back from Bucharest, and she brought with her a quilted vest.
5.   My aunt came back from Montreal, and she brought with her a parasol.
6.   My aunt came back from old Beijing, and she brought with her a golden ring.
7.   My aunt came back from Mandalay, and she brought with her a red beret.
8.   Now my aunt's going off to Kathmandu., but this time—she's taking me too!

Or:

1–4 the same as above

5.   My aunt came back from Kalamazoo, and she brought with her some gum to chew.
6.   My aunt came back from Niagra Falls and brought with her some ping pong balls.
7.   My aunt came back from the New York Fair, and she brought with her a rocking chair.
8.   My aunt came back from near Kamloops, and she brought with her some hula hoops.
9.   My aunt came back from the Hebribes, and brought with her some itchy fleas.
10. My aunt came back from Timbuktu, and brought with her some nuts like you!

Movement Directions:

1.   Sing the song adding a motion for each verse. (There are lots of variations on verses.) Here are a few key words you might use: Tap foot for shoe, wave a pretend fan, make scissor motion for shears, pretend to chew gum, head moves up and down as your eyes follow a ping pong ball, rock body as if in a rocking chair, twirl hips for hula hoop motion, point to other children on nuts like you!
2.   This is a cumulative song - Continue doing all motions as you add new ones. This gets more complicated, silly and fun.

Noble Duke of York

Singing Game from England

Oh the No - ble Duke of York he
had ten thous - and men. He marched them up to the
top of the hill and he marched them down a - gain.

Game directions: Class forms a long ways set, facing partners.

1. Forward three steps and pause. Backward three steps and pause. (2x)
2. Head couple sashays down the set and back.
3. Head couple casts off down the outside of the set. (Peel the banana.)
4. Head couple makes an arch at the bottom (holding both hands).
5. Both lines go under the arch and back to place.
6. Begin again with a new head couple.

Nobody Likes Me

2. Down goes the first one, down goes the second one, oh, how they wiggle and squirm.
   Long, thin, slimy ones, short, fat, juicy ones, Itsy, bitsy, fuzzy, wuzzy worms.
3. Up comes the first one, up comes the second one, oh, how they wiggle and squirm.
   Long, thin, slimy ones, short, fat, juicy ones, Itsy, bitsy, fuzzy, wuzzy worms.

Oh Susanna

Stephen Foster

Oh, When the Saints

Old Brass Wagon

2. Circle to the right, ...
3. All go in, ... all come out, ...

Old MacDonald

Folk song

2. Pig—oink, oink
3. Turkey—gobble, gobble
4. Chicken—cluck, cluck
5. Cow—moo, moo
6. Cat—meow, meow
7. Mule—Hee haw
8. Dog—bow wow

Pin Pon (in Spanish)

Folk Song from Latin America

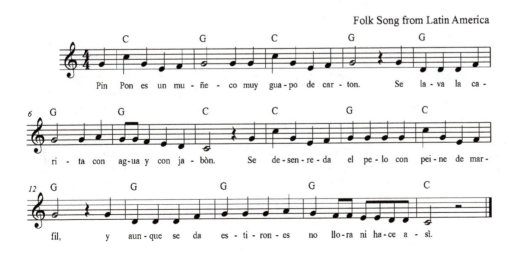

2. Cuando toma la sopa no ensucia el delantal, Pues come con cuidado parece un general. Y cuando las estsrellas empiezan a brillar, Pin Pon se va a la cama se a cuesta a descansar.

3. Pin Pon's my little puppet, he's handsome and he's good; He uses soap and water to wash just as he should. He has a brush and comb just to make his hair look neat. And if he pulls it hard, he still doesn't make a peep.

4. Pin Pon joins me for dinner; he is a welcome guest; He sips his soup so nicely and doesn't make a mess. When nighttime comes upon us and stars are twinkling bright, Pin Pon gets in his bed and I hear him say, "Good night."

Pizza-Pizza Daddy-O

Singing Game

This can be sung while jumping rope, or turned in to a game where children make up more motions after singing "Let's rope it, rope it rope it, daddy-o"
Add "Let's swim it" "Let's twist it" "Let's dance it", etc. until ending with "Let's end it daddy-o"

Rain, Rain Go Away

Traditional

Rocky Mountain

Traditional

2. Sunny valley, sunny valley, sunny valley low. When you're in that sunny valley, sing it soft and slow.
   (Chorus)
3. Stormy ocean, stormy ocean, stormy ocean wide. When you're on that deep blue sea, there's no place you can hide.
   (Chorus)

Row, Row, Row Your Boat

Traditional

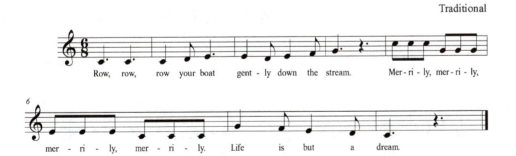

Sakura

Japanese Folk Song

Sally Go 'Round the Sun

Traditional Rhyme

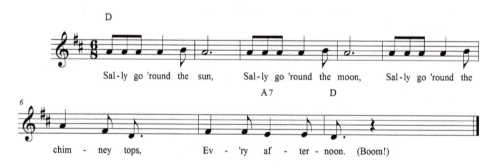

Scotland's Burning

Traditional

Se, Se, Se (Japan)

Japenese Game Song

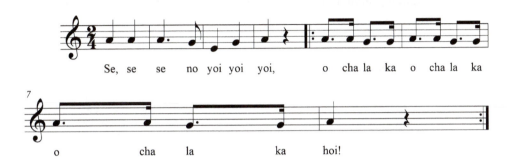

Se, se se no yoi yoi yoi,   o cha la ka o cha la ka

o   cha la   ka   hoi!

Game Directions:

Point out the origin of the song and make a cross curricular connection, asking, "What do you know about the country of Japan?" Discuss bowing as a cultural way to show respect for others.

1. Teach song by rote.
2. As they sing, have children pound the steady beat with a fist into the palm of the other hand.
3. Demonstrate the surprise at the end of the song. On the last word, show paper, rock, or scissors sign. By doing this on the beat, it is much easier for children to play fairly and not switch symbols.
4. Have children stand with partners. Bow to each other at the beginning of the game as if to say, "I will be a good sport, play fairly and value you as someone I respect."
5. Sing the song, keeping the beat and showing rock, paper, scissors. If there is a tie, repeat singing the last phrase and playing. Keep repeating until there is a winner.
6. The winner of the game raises hand in air and wiggles fingers. The other partner bows again as a way to say, "Thank you for playing with me."

End of game Options:

1. Everyone changes partners and plays again and again until teacher calls time.
2. Put winners on one side of the room and play again. Keep winners and play again until one child is the class champion. Give the winner a sticker and put everyone back in the game. This goes fast so several children could win stickers in one session, Everyone else keeps practicing on one side of the room.

See Saw

Traditional

See   saw   up   and down.   In   the   air   and   on   the ground.

Game directions:

Formation—seated circle with partners facing each other.

Partners are seated with knees up and toes/shoes touching.

Holding both of partner's hands.

Children sing the song while rocking back and forth simulating a see saw motion.

At the end of the song, children turn and face the opposite direction and continue game with new partner.

Shake Them Simmons Down

Game Song from Texas

2. Circle left, ... Shake them 'simmons down.
3. Boys to the center, ... Shake them 'simmons down.
4. Girls to the center, ... Shake them 'simmons down.
5. Promenade all, ... Shake them 'simmons down.
6. Swing your corner, ... Shake them 'simmons down.

She'll Be Coming 'Round the Mountain

Southern Mountain Song

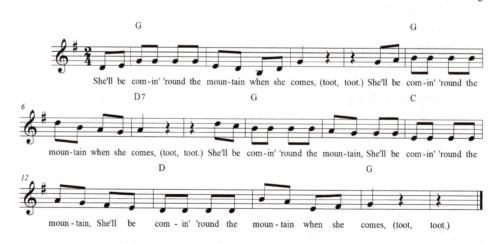

1. She'll be comin' 'round the mountain when she comes, toot, toot—beep horn
2. She'll be driving six white horses when she comes, whoa back!—pull back the reins of a horse
3. Oh, we'll all go out to greet her when she comes, "Hi babe!"—hand wave
4. Oh, we'll all have chicken and dumplings when she comes, yum, yum—rub stomach
5. Oh, she'll have to sleep with Grandma when she comes, snore, snore!—sleeping head on hands and snoring sounds.

Shoheen Sho

Welsh Folk Song

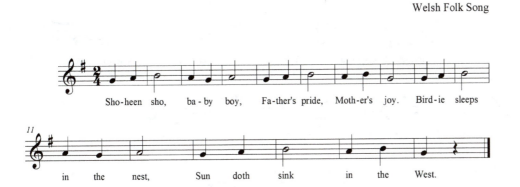

2. Shoheen sho, baby girl. Father's pride, Mother's pearl.
   Birdie sleeps in the nest, Sun doth sink in the West.
3. Shoheen sho, little dove, Fill my heart full of love.
   Birdie sleeps in the nest, Sun doth sink in the West.

Skip to my Lou

Traditional Frontier Song

The Star Spangled Banner

John Stafford Smith

In 1814, Francis Scott Key wrote the poem, Defense of Fort McHenry. The poem was later set to the tune of The Anacreontic Song by John Stafford Smith, though somewhat modified and retitled to The Star Spangled Banner. The U.S. Congress proclaimed The Star Spangled Banner the U.S. National Anthem in 1931.

2. On the shore dimly seen through the mists of the deep. Where the foe's haughty host in dread silence reposes. What is that which the breeze, o'er the towering steep, as it fitfully blows, half conceals, half discloses? Now it catches the gleam of the morning's first beam, in full glory reflected, now shines on the stream: 'Tis the star spangled banner: O, long may it wave O'er the land of the free and the home of the brave!

3. And where is that band who so vauntingly swore that the havoc of war and the battle's confusion a home and a country should leave us no more? Their blood has wash'd out their foul footsteps/pollution. No refuge could save the hireling and slave from the terror of flight or the gloom of the grave: And the star

spangled banner in triumph doth wave O'er the land of the free and the home of the brave.

4. O, thus be it ever when freemen shall stand, Between their lov'd homes and the war's desolation; Blest with vict'ry and peace, may the heav'n-rescued land Praise the Pow'r that hath made and preserv'd us a nation! Then conquer we must, when our cause is just, And this be our motto: "In God is our trust" And the star spangled banner in triumph shall wave O'er the land of the free and the home of the brave!

Sweet Betsy From Pike

American Ballad

Swing Low, Sweet Chariot

Spiritual

Texas, Our Texas

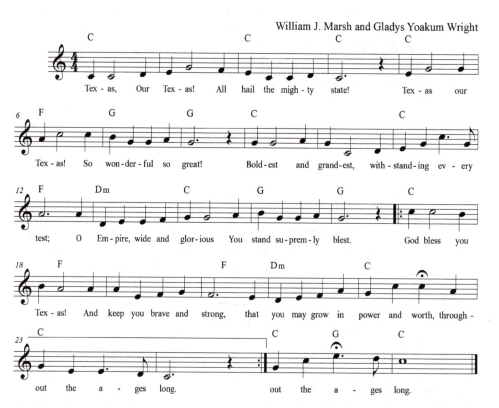

William J. Marsh and Gladys Yoakum Wright

Tex - as, Our Tex - as! All hail the migh - ty state! Tex - as our

Tex - as! So won - der - ful so great! Bold - est and grand - est, with - stand - ing ev - ery

test; O Em - pire, wide and glor - ious You stand su - prem - ly blest. God bless you

Tex - as! And keep you brave and strong, that you may grow in power and worth, through -

out the a - ges long.   out the a - ges long.

2. Texas, O Texas! Your freeborn single star, sends out its radiance to nations near and far. Emblem of Freedom! it sets our hearts aglow, with thoughts of San Jacinto and glorious Alamo.
   (Chorus)
3. Texas, dear Texas! from tyrant grip now free, shines forth in splendor, your star of destiny! Mother of heroes, we come your children true, proclaiming our allegiance, our faith, our love for you.
   (Chorus)

This official Texas state song was adopted by the legislature in 1929 after being selected in a state-wide competition. The tune was composed by William J. Marsh and the lyrics were written by William Marsh and Gladys Yoakum Wright. In 1929 Texas was the largest state in the union and the word Boldest was Largest. When Alaska became a state in 1959, Texas could no longer make the claim of being the largest and the lyrics were changed.

The Rattlin' Bog

Irish Traditional

O - ro, the rat - tlin' bog, and the bog down in the val - ley - o,

O - ro, the rat - tlin' bog, and the bog down in the val - ley - o, and in that bog there was a tree, a

rare tree, and a rat - tlin' tree, tree in the bog [_____] and the bog down in the val - ley - o.

(See lesson plan in chapter 8 for instrument and movement ideas to add after singing.)

2. And on that tree there was a limb, a rare limb, a rattlin' limb. A limb on the tree and the tree in the bog and the bog down in the valley-o.
   (Chorus)
3. And on that limb there was a branch . . .
   (Chorus)
4. And on that branch there was a nest . . .
   (Chorus)
5. And in that nest there was an egg . . .
   (Chorus)
6. And in that egg there was a bird . . .
   (Chorus)

Optional verses:

And on that bird there was tail . . .
And on that tail there was a feather . . .
Make up your own verses from here.

Tideo

Play-Party Song from Texas

Pass one win-dow, Ti-de-o, Pass two win-dows, Ti-de-o. Pass three win-dows, Ti-de-o,

Jin-gle at the win-dow, Ti-de-o. Ti-de-o, Ti-de-o, Jin-gle at the win-dow Ti-de-o.

Game Directions:

Formation—Double circle, facing partners

Outside circle steps to the right on the word "**pass**" and can pretend to wash the window/or wave goodbye.

Partners wave both hands in the air on "jingle at the window Tideo".

Partners right arm turn on "Tideo, Tideo".

The Old Gray Cat

Folk Song

Game Directions:

Clear a space for all to play. Choose one child to be a cat, all other children are the mice. Decide where the opening would be for the mouse hole. Any child behind and in the mouse hole is "safe". The cat pretends to be asleep in the middle of the room. On verse 2, the mice leave the mouse hole and creep past the cat to the other side of the space. On verse 3 they stop and pretend to nibble the cheese. The mice remain there until verse 5. On verse 4, the cat wakes up, stretches and creeps back and forth not going not going near the mice. Verse 5, the tempo of the song becomes allegro and the mice all quickly scamper (still on their hands and knees) back to the mouse hole. The cat tries to tag and tap as many mice as possible, (still on his/her hands and knees). Everyone that is tagged becomes a cat and the game song begins again.

2. The little mice are creeping . . . .
3. The little mice are nibbling . . .
4. The old gray cat is creeping . . .
5. The little mice all scamper . . .

This Land is Your Land

Woody Guthrie

1. As I was walking that ribbon of highway, I saw above me that endless skyway. I saw below me that golden valley, This land was made for you and me.

2. I've roamed and rambled and I followed my footsteps to the sparkling sands of her diamond deserts, And all around me a voice was sounding, "This land was made for you and me."

3. When the sun comes shining and I was strolling and the wheat fields waving and the dust clouds rolling, As the fog was lifting a voice was chanting, "This land was made for you and me."

This Old Man

English Folk Song

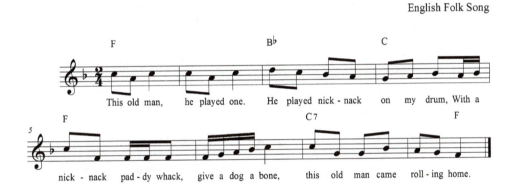

Train Is A Comin'

African-American Spiritual

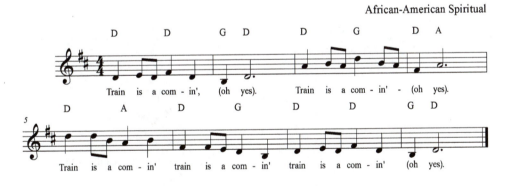

Trot Old Joe

Texas Folk Song

2. Walk, Old Joe, walk, Old Joe, You ride better'n any horse I know, ...
3. Gallop, Old Joe, . . .
4. Jump, Old Joe, . . .

Way Down Yonder in the Brickyard

Traditional Game Song, Georgia Sea Island Singers

We Are Playing in the Forest

Traditional Melody

Game directions:

Choose one student to be the wolf.

All other students walk through the forest while singing the song.

Stop at the end of the song and say, "Wolf are you there?"

The wolf has a choice of answering, "No, I'm _____ ." (Answer choices could be, "No, I'm combing my hair", "I'm brushing my teeth" etc. Be creative!). The game begins again.

If the answer is, "Yes!" the wolf tags someone close to them who becomes the next wolf.

Suggestion—set up a limit on how many times the wolf can say no. In a small classroom set up where there is not much space to move, try putting chairs in a circle with one less chair than children in the forest.

What Shall We Do on a Rainy Day?

Traditional Melody

Yonder Come Day

Spiritual

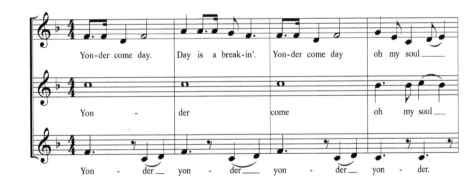

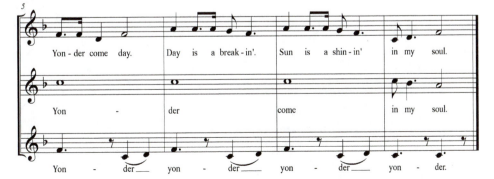

You Are My Sunshine

Jimmie Davis and Charles Mitchell

ADDITIONAL ENGAGING ACTIVITIES

EXTENDING THE FORM OF A SINGING GAME—FOR PRIMARY GRADES

1. Extend a singing game by combining movement and symphonic music to create an ABA form for performance.

- *Charlie Over the Ocean; Aquarium from Carnival of the Animals* by C. Saint-Saens

Process:

Song

Sing entire song before asking the students to echo by phrase. Yes, I know this is an echo song but they don't know that.

Accompaniment

Have students sing while you use speech to layer in one ostinato—start with the BX (Bass Xylophone) part. Use levels to show the chord change. Then divide class in half and have one part sing while the other half recites the ostinato using speech.

Then switch. Transfer the speech to a simple body percussion.

Perform then transfer to the pitched percussion. This will help students to hear how the ostinati fits in—subdivision. Do this for each ostinato.

Singing Game Movement

Choose a theme: i.e., things found in the ocean.

Go around the circle and have students name something found in the ocean.

Have students in a seated circle with "it" on the outside singing the phrase while the circle sings the repeat/echo.

Have students patch on the chase section while the pitched instruments play rapidly, but gently on the box or on the floor.

Listening Selection: *Aquarium from Carnival of the Animals* by C. Saint-Saens.
See the lesson in Chapter 7, Engaging Children with Movement

Putting it all together!

Create a form: ABA or others . . . .

Have students create a speech introduction which could include names of oceans, seas, fish, etc. Incorporate the *Aquarium* section.

Review form of piece—have a student write it on the board.

2. Combine language, music, and movement for performance.

- Objective: To have the students identify Rondo form.

TEKS: 1.1 Perception. The student describes and analyzes musical sound and demonstrates musical artistry.
C. The student is expected to identify repetition and contrast in musical examples. Creative Expression/Performance. The student performs a varied repertoire of music.

Materials: "Thunder, Lightning, Rain, Rain" (see Chapter 2, Engaging Children with Rhythm); "Rain, Rain"; "Who Built the Ark"; *Rondeau* from Symphonie de Fanfares by Mouret; pictures of brass instruments; rondo 'chart' on board.

Process:

Teach the poem "Thunder, Lightning, Rain, Rain"

Thunder, lightning, rain, rain.
Water down the drain, drain.
Sunshine brings it back again.
Thunder, lightning, rain, rain.

Review the sol-mi song "Rain, Rain".

Students insert their own name on ". . . little _____ wants to play."

New Song: "Who Built the Ark"

Students keep a beat while teacher sings the song. Ask students, "What does this song have in common with the other song and rhyme?" Learn the song by using the rote process.

Have students insert the poem before each song they have learned. This will create a rondo form for performance.

Learn a hand clapping pattern.

Practice a simple patty cake pattern while reciting the poem, "*Thunder, Lightning, Rain, Rain*".

Practicing the rondo form

- Stand still and sing "Rain, Rain"
- Continue with "Thunder, Lightning"
- Stand still on "Who Built the Ark?"
- End with "Thunder, Lightning"
- Map form on the board.

Additional or optional activities:

- Have students hold one hand and skip throughout the room singing "Rain, Rain".
- Have students skip solo throughout the room singing "Who Built the Ark/"
- Now have the students insert the A section "Thunder, Lightning".
- Perform the Rain Rondo.
- Review the instruments of the Brass family with picture charts.
- Listen to "Rondeau" by Mouret. Have students identify the returning section of the rondo by raising their hand.
- Check for understanding: have students transfer their movements from the "Rain Rondo" to the "Rondeau".

Evaluation: Could the students change to each section without the teacher's help?

3. Spin Me a Story

Creating Drama with Core Songs and Speech Pieces

Happiness
Objective: To have the students create a mini musical incorporating *Happiness; Rain, Rain;* sports activities and rondo form.

Materials: Speech piece Happiness; s-m song Rain, Rain; BX; AX; SG; AG; drum; cymbal; guiro; rachet.

Procedure:
Review Happiness: by A.A. Milne
Speech with beat on lap
transfer "John" to "C1" on barred instruments
play bordun C1–G1 on beat while reciting rhyme
have metals play only "John" on C1 while woods play the bordun on C1–G1
add melody

Start spinning the story: (some students are seated at barred instruments—others play John)

Once there was a boy named John who liked to play outdoors after school . . . . . It didn't matter what the weather was like outside. One day it started to rain. First one drop (barred instruments), then another . . . . . (Review *Rain, Rain*). Just then the back door opened (rachet) and John heard his mother say . . . . . But John didn't listen; he kept playing with his friends. Just then an amazing thing happened. The back door opened (rachet) and out came John's waterproof boots (drum) . . . . . (*Happiness*—words to "waterproof boots" then "loo" the rest).

John put on the boots and continued to play . . . . . until he heard the back door open (rachet) and his mother say . . . . . But John didn't listen; he kept playing with his friends. Just then an amazing thing happened. The back door opened (rachet) and out came John's waterproof hat (cymbal) appeared . . . . . (*Happiness*—words to "waterproof hat" then "loo" the rest).

John put on the hat and continued to play . . . . . until he heard the back door open (rachet) and his mother say . . . . . But John didn't listen; he kept playing with his friends. Just then an amazing thing happened. The back door opened (rachet) and out came John's waterproof Macintosh (guiro) . . . . . (*Happiness*—words to "waterproof Macintosh and.." "said John").

Movement: Have all students come to the center and discuss and pantomime various sports/games John and his friends could play. Decide on a game or games.

Storyboard: Notate the form. Assign parts. Perform.

Evaluation: Did all students participate and have opportunities for input in the story? Did the students follow their story map?

Dances from Around the World

Line Dance—No Partners

Pata Pata—South African—Miriam Makeba
Formation: blocked for line dance formation

Rt. Ft. Touch step, Lft. Ft. Touch step
Toes out, heels out; toes in, heels in
Rt. Knee lift up down; up down
Clap; step and turn 2, 3, 4

Line Dance—No Partners/Groups

Cotton Eyed Joe
Formation: line dance formation
Part A: Cross rt. Foot over lt. Foot/Kick out rt. Foot
Step backward rt. Lt. rt.
Cross lt. Foot over rt. Foot/Kick out lt. foot
Step backward lt. Rt. lt.
Cross rt. Foot over lt. Foot/Kick out rt. Foot
Step backward rt. Lt. rt.
Cross lt. Foot over rt. Foot/Kick out lt. foot
Step backward lt. Rt. lt.
Part B: Shuffle forward: rt. lt. rt./lt. rt. lt./rt. lt. rt./lt. rt. lt./   rt. lt. rt./lt. rt. lt./
rt. lt. rt./lt. rt. lt./

Circle Dance With Partners—Mixer

La Raspa a Dance Mixer from Mexico
Formation: a double circle of partners facing each other
Part A: Hands on own waist; bleking step/leaping from heel to heel
4 X Heel, heel, heel clap/clap
Part B:
16 beats: link arms and turn a whole circle;
16 beats: change arms and turn a whole circle in the other direction. Outside person moves one space to the right (now you have a new partner) clockwise

Circle Dance with Partners–Mixer

Fjaskern—Swedish
Formation: Partners in double circle facing counterclockwise.
Focus: locomotor to nonlocomotor movement; progressive dance.
p. 192 in TMD RM CD 2:9
Part I: Forward (15 beats), turn, forward (clockwise)(16 beats)

Part 2: Bleking step, 2,3,4; change, 2,3,4
Repeat this section 3 times

Troika–Folk Dance Mixer from Russia

Formation: groups of 3 partners standing shoulder to shoulder; handing hands up to shoulder height; facing counter clockwise—visualize spokes in a wagon wheel.

Part A: kicking step or jogging step 16 steps forward (counter clockwise).

Part B: numbering from inside being #1, middle person is #2 and outside person is #3. Without dropping hands #3 travels under arm of #1 (#2 follows under and back to center). Without dropping hands #1 travels under arm of #3 (#3 follows under and back to center).

Part C: #1 and #3 connect the circle. Jogging, circle left 12 steps; with feet together hop diagonally heels left, right, left.
Jogging, circle right 12 steps; straighten out line; #2 moves forward to the next group.

Circle Dance–No Partners

Farandole
Objective: To re-create a popular historical dance from Medieval times.
Materials: Recorder and hand drum or "Two Tunes to Dance By" CD track 1; *Polanaise* from Shenanigans CD.
Dance Vocabulary: *Serpent, Thread the Needle, Escargot #1 & #2, Tree Trunk.*
Formation: Partners in a single line/open circle. Music: 6/8

- *Serpent*
- *Thread the Needle*
- *Escargot #1 then #2*
- *Tree trunk*

Evaluation: Were the students able to lead the dance? Were the transitions into the various figures smooth? Compare and contrast the dance styles in the Grand March versus Farandole.

Note: I teach the Farandole during the Texas Renaissance Festival months in the fall.
See: English Folk Music (to Abbots Bromley Horn Dance)

Circle Dance–No Partners

Zemer Atik—Israel
Formation: Circle facing counterclockwise, L hand at shoulder, R arm straight, hands joined.

Focus: Specified foot; counterclockwise; in to out; hand movements
p. 186 Teaching Movement and Dance RM CD 4: 7
Part I: Forward, 2, 3, 4; Forward/clap; Forward/clap, clap (Weikart uses 1 clap here)
Repeat three times.
Part 2: In/snap, in/snap, out, 2, 3, 4
Repeat three times.

Circle Dance No Partners

Ya Abud—Arabic Men's Dance

Choreographed by Moshiko—1974

Formation: Open circle facing in, standing shoulder to shoulder, arms down, hold hands or pinky fingers.
Part 1: side/close to the right [small steps, stiff legs with slight bouncing]
Part 2: right foot stomp, in in, stomp stomp, out out; 2 stomps, in in, stomp stomp, out out
Part 3: right foot swing, swing, swing, step step
Part 4: facing counterclockwise diagonal; rock back and forth while moving to the right.
Part 5: chug with both feet, knees bent: in, out/out, in, out/out
Part 6: side, side, cross rt. Foot over; side, side cross lt. foot over
Part 7: walk facing counter clockwise; hands joined and held shoulder height [length of steps—"Walla, Walla, Washington, is not a place I want to be"]

Partners in a Long Ways Set—Not a Mixer

Grand March
Objective: To perform dances from various periods of time and from a variety of cultures.
Materials: CD player; any reel or jig.: Any 32 bar jig or reel for the Grand March such as those on the *Permanent Wave CD*.
Focus: Follow the leader formations. No specified foot.
Dance vocabulary: *cast off, arch, escargot, spiral.*
Formation: Partners facing up the set, holding inside hands.
Procedure:

1. Walk through the figures below untimed—no music.
    *   Cast off, follow the leader, make arch at bottom of the set, follow through making arches.
    *   Head couple walks single file through the arch, forming a single line.
    *   Escargot formation. Tight spiral—cut through the spiral, go under the last person's hands.
    *   Escargot formation. Tight spiral—reverse the spiral.
    *   Form arches.
    *   Cast off in pairs, meeting at the bottom, coming back in 4's.
    *   Cast off in 4's, coming back in 8's, etc. until a circle is formed.

2. Now add the music which will time the steps.

Evaluation: Were the students able to lead the dance? Were the transitions into the various figures smooth?
Note: I use the Grand March for parent participation at PTA/PTO open house meetings.

Contra Dance/Long Ways Set–Mixer

Yankee Doodle—Early American (ca. 1775)
Contra Dance, Music: *Yankee Doodle* Dance Source: The Colonial Music Institute
(*Bringing History to Life Through Music*)
Formation: Longways set
Language: hands 4 from the top; actives/inactives; star right; star left; down the center;
turn alone; cast off.
Personal body stance: stand tall, ribcage up; lead with the chest; when dancing have eye
contact with your partner; have direction/purpose when moving.

Procedures:

- History of *Yankee Doodle*
- Execute each figure untimed
- Execute each figure to a specified beat
- Listen to a clip of the music for tempo
- Perform *Yankee Doodle* to the music

A. Star right (8 counts)
   Star left (8 counts)

B. Actives (1's) down the center (6 counts); turn alone (drop hands and turn
   towards each other and resume hand hold) (2 counts)
   come back (6 counts); cast around the inactives (2's) (2 counts).

Note: Check out The Colonial Music Institute site at www.colonialmusic.org/Resource/
howtoCD.html and The University of Oklahoma Law Center site at www.law.ou.edu/
hist/yankee.html for research on Yankee Doodle.

Contra Dance/Long Ways Set–Mixer

Jefferson Reel—*Early American (ca.1801)*
Contra Dance, Music any 2-part reel.
Formation: Longways set
Music: Permanent Wave CD
Language: Hands 4 from the top; actives/inactives; circle right; circle left; star right;
star left; actives down the outside; line of 4; pop through.

Procedures:
Execute each figure untimed
Execute each figure to a specified beat
Listen to a clip of the music for tempo
Perform Jefferson Reel to the music

A1 Circle left (8 counts)
   Circle right (8 counts)

A2 Star right (8 counts)
   Star left (8 counts)

B1 Actives (1's) down the outside (8 counts)
Come home (8 counts)

B2 Actives in the middle for a line of 4 (8 counts)
Come back home—inactives pop through the middle into the next set (move the set toward the top—8 counts)

Additional Cross Curricular Ideas

Curricular Integrations—Language Arts

"Who Fed the after Chickens" (Pronouns), Peter and the Wolf and The Nutcracker (Parts of the Story), Hot Cross Buns (sequencing), Bernie Bee (writing a story), Rattlin' Bog https://youtu.be/jaAcC_Sk-Vc.

Curricular Integrations—Science

Seashell (identify and describe natural sources of water) Frosty Weather and Vivaldi's Four Seasons (identify characteristics of the seasons; record weather information) Each of Us is a Flower (identify parts of the plants) https://youtu.be/ORA9pzKDgbs.

Science of Sound

- Acoustics: The science of sound
- Musical Acoustics: Scientific aspects of musical tones, including sound waves, timbre, pitch, intervals, scales, and tone production, as well as the behavior or sound waves within a given space or room
- Complex Tones: The combination of the strong fundamental and higher overtones
- Harmonics: the overtones accompanying a fundamental tone at a fixed interval

Science of Sound for Children

- Vibration: All sounds, including music, originate from the vibration of an object. Sound waves must travel through a medium.
- Sound happens in waves that travel out from the origin of the sound and can be bounced back, creating an echo.
- Frequency determines the pitch of a sound wave.
- Sound waves can be heard by the human ear because of its particular anatomy.

Homemade Instruments

- Explore the science of sound
- Remember the following concepts:

The size of the instrument makes a difference in pitch. How does an instrument vibrate to produce sound? How can you manipulate the instrument to change its pitch? Experiment with tubes, bottles, rubber bands, etc. Remember, an instrument needs vibration and a resonating chamber to amplify the sound.

Curricular Integrations—Math

- Two Four Six Eight (Grouping Numbers), Wishy Washy (Multiplication), Weevily Wheat (Multiplication).

Curricular Integration—Social Studies

- Geography Rocky Mountain (Landforms), I Love the Mountains (Landforms), Grand Canyon Suite, (Landforms) https://youtu.be/6_7DA1G6tVs.

Curricular Integration—Technology

- BrainBreaks: Go Noodle! And The Learning Station.
- Music Informational Websites: Look for kids sites on city orchestra websites.
- Interactive Websites: Hansel and Gretel Opera.
- Garage Band and Audacity to create loops and arrangements.
- iPad apps for learning various instruments or practicing ear training.

Curricular Integrations—Art

Flashlight Dancing—Make your room as dark as possible for this game.

1. Teacher chooses a song with a variety of tempo and dynamic changes.
2. Discuss warm and cool colors on the color wheel. Discuss how colors could also suggest the mood and tempos of music.
3. Have each student bring a flashlight from home. Using a rubber band and attach a small square of colored cellophane to the top of the light.
4. Ask children to lay down on the floor looking up at the ceiling.
5. As the music plays, ask students to shine their flashlight colors and move to the beat of the music. Teacher may call out specific colors that fit certain sections of the music.

CREATE A SCHOOL MUSIC PROGRAM

Do you remember performing in a school play or musical in elementary school? Describe your experience. _____

_____

_____

Many times a principal will ask a grade level or teacher to have students perform at a PTA meeting, a school celebration, or holiday. Parents love to see their children on stage and take lots of photos of their children demonstrating what they have learned in school. Pulling together a program is fun and exciting! Here are some suggested steps to make it a success.

1. Form production team (Principal approval, fellow team teachers, grade level teachers, front office staff, custodial staff, parents, high school helpers, community members)
2. Create budget (Do you need to fundraise, ask for donations, or is there budget money available?)
3. Choose a theme and show title. "NASA in Space," "Major Metric and the Power of Ten," "Coming to America," "Mother's Day Celebration," "Texas Hoedown" etc. Be very sensitive to your students and choose your subject matter wisely.
4. List Music and Integrated Subject objectives that will be covered in this show.
5. Target grade level and students involved. Think about how all children can be included and many different parts can be assigned that will make every child feel important and give each one a chance at the spotlight. Elementary shows are not designed to show off the talents of one particular child but to show everyone's best efforts.
6. Write Script leaving a blank where a singing a song would be appropriate.
7. Choose Songs with an accompaniment tracks or plan to have an accompanist. Write the song titles on the script.
8. Create Movement/Instrument parts. Decide if you would like to have movement to some of the songs to engage the children and write out your plan. Instruments can be added to songs or have a small ensemble play a simple song during transition times.
9. Plan backdrop/props/scenery for the stage. Ask the art teacher or enlist volunteers to help. Be as simple or detailed as you want. It all adds to the overall effect.
10. Create costumes—If you have a school T-shirt, three mothers that can sew or a big budget that lets you order from a catalog, adding costumes will bring your show to life. A paper hat for Abraham Lincoln is just as good as a real one. Let students help create costume pieces in class.
11. Print a program for parents (include thank you and acknowledgements)

When all of that is decided and approved by your Principal, it's time to teach.

11. Create lesson plans for instruction—Decide the number of lessons needed to learn all the songs and how many weeks are needed to complete the production.
12. Arrange for final rehearsals on stage. Who will play the CD? Arrange pianist or sound engineer. Do you need a sound system and microphones for speakers and solo/ensemble singers? Do you need help hanging the backdrop or setting up risers?
13. PERFORM!

Sample Script
This is a third-grade show performed on Veteran's Day. If you wish to use it, change the songs to ones that are available to you. Assign the parts as needed.

George Washington: American Veteran

Script by Laura McGregor

Source books:
Our Country's Founders by William J. Bennett
When Washington Crossed the Delaware by Lynne Cheney
George Did It by Suzanne Tripp Jurmain
George Washington by James Cross Giblin

Third-Grade **insert name of choir** enters marching and playing rhythm instruments to "The Stars and Stripes Forever" by John Philip Sousa

Student 1 _____ Welcome to our third-grade musical show, "George Washington: American Veteran."
Student 2. _____ The third-grade "Cougar Chorus" is proud to perform for you. (All bow)
Student 3 _____ We ask that all cell phones, pagers, and small children be turned to vibrate.
Student 4 _____ George Washington, American Veteran! The Father of Our Country!
We salute him and all of our veterans who have kept our country safe and free.
Student 5. _____ I know that George Washington is the "Father of our Country" but to be "honest", I really don't know that much about him.
Student 1. _____ We can help. Give me a beat maestro and we'll sing you a song with the first 3 important facts to remember.
SING: Who is on a Dollar Bill? By Teresa Jennings

(Continue assigning speaking parts)

1. Let's review. Who is on a dollar bill? (Audience: George Washington)
2. Who is on a quarter? (Audience: George Washington)
3. Who was our first President? (Audience: George Washington)
4. Great! By Jove, I think you've got it!
5. But wait, there's more. Did you recognize that famous picture of George on the dollar bill? That portrait was by the famous American painter, Gilbert Stuart.
6. If you take a trip to the Smithsonian Museum in Washington D.C., you can see this amazing portrait in person.
7. I'd love to see that! (Turn to audience) Mom, can I go this summer? Please?

If you go, you can stop by George Washington's home in nearby Virginia. It's a farm called Mount Vernon.
8. The house is on a hill that overlooks the Potomac River. It is a beautiful place and has been preserved for all generations to see his home.
9. George started out his life as a farm boy. He learned about growing crops, fishing in the river, riding horses, and working hard to survive.
10. He was always taller than his friends. He was growing into size 13 shoes and eventually was going to 6 feet, two inches tall.
11. Most men at that time averaged 5 feet, 7 inches in height. That's a big difference.
12. Much later, his wife, Martha, had a big bed made just for him so his feet wouldn't stick out over the end.

13. There wasn't a school for George and they didn't want to send him back to England to go to school, so his parents hired a local minister to teach him how to read and write and do sums.

14. George had a hard time with spelling.

15. The story of George taking a little hatchet and chopping up everything in his Father's garden, including a cherry tree has been told for generations.

16. When his Father asked, "Who chopped down my cherry tree?," George was honest and said, "I cannot tell a lie, Father. It was I."

17. His Father was so happy George told the truth; he hugged him and forgave him.

18. Wait! I thought that was a story, . . . fiction, . . . not true.

19. Well, to be "honest" I don't think we really know. What we do know is that George Washington was a man of great character.

20. He was a man every American trusted. He was honest and dependable.

21. When we needed someone to lead our country, manage our government, appoint the judges, approve the laws, command the troops, take charge of the nation's money, and make friends with foreign countries, everyone agreed George could do it!

Sing: George Washington by Teresa Jennings

1. One of the most important things you should know about George Washington was that he was our country's first Veteran because he was the first general in charge of the America's first army.

2. The year was 1775 and the 13 American colonies asked George to be commander in chief of the brand new colonial army.

3. It was hard to make real soldiers out of volunteer tradesmen, shopkeepers and farmers, but George did it.

4. When war broke out, America asked George and his soldiers to fight the mighty British army so that the 13 colonies could be free. That job took almost 8 long hard years, but George did it.

5. One of the great turning points of the Revolutionary War was the American victory at the Battle of Trenton.

6. The war had not been going well for the American army and it looked like the rebellion was coming to a quick end.

7. George wrote a letter to his brother which said, "You can form no idea of the perplexity of my situation. No man, I believe, has ever had a greater choice of difficulties and less means to extricate himself from them. However, under a full persuasion of the justice of our cause I cannot entertain an idea that it will finally sink, though it may remain for some time under a cloud."

8. When the struggle seemed hopeless, George Washington did not give up. He called a meeting of his generals and worked out his plan.

9. So, General Washington planned a surprise attack on Christmas day, 1776, but it was winter, extremely cold and they had to cross a frozen river.

10. Many of the soldiers did not have jackets to keep them warm. Many had no shoes and marched with rags wrapped around their feet. Everyone was hungry, sick, exhausted and cold.

11. The 2400 men crowded into the large black boats and tried to navigate across the river.

12. The river was swirling with frozen chunks of ice that threatened to capsize the boats. Crossing the Delaware with men, horses, and cannon was extremely dangerous and treacherous.
13. They made it, but still had 9 miles to march through a storm of frozen sleet and snow.
14. These men loved their country and their leader. The surprise worked and the Americans won the battle! Under George Washington's command, they turned the tide of the war and changed the course of history.
15. These 1st American veterans were heroes, full of persistence and patriotism!
16. To honor their sacrifice, we sing the official song of the Army, composed by Gen. Edmund Gruber. The song describes the willingness of our Army to go anywhere they are needed to protect us all.

Sing: The Caissons Go Rolling Along by Gen Gruber

1. And the caissons go rolling along, keep 'em rolling, ... Hey what is a caisson?
2. It's actually the box of ammunition on the cannon cart with wheels. The horses would pull it along as the army marched to where they needed to go.
3. Today the army has changed the words to "The Army goes rolling along". Anyway you sing it, it's got a catchy tune! But, back to George Washington. What happened after that battle?
4. General Washington and his men had stood with their country in a time of crisis.

When they were cold and hungry, they did not quit. When the conflict was hard, they fought on.

5. When they won, the victory was sweet. News of Trenton and Princeton spread across the land, lifting the spirits of patriots everywhere. Now all Americans could imagine that their great struggle would have a glorious end.
6. And it did. The Revolutionary War was won and America was the first country to truly have a democracy and freedom.
7. Today, America still has struggles to keep our country safe and free and we owe all of our veterans a great debt of gratitude and thanks.
8. Some of our (insert name of school and mascot) have family members serving in the military now. We would like to thank them. Please stand if you are with us tonight and would their families please stand as well?

(Read list and then lead applause). Please remain standing and if there are any other veterans in our audience would you please join them? (Lead applause again.)

9. Thank you. You may be seated. We will never forget our friends and family who are serving in the military and are far from home. Our heartfelt wish and our final song is "Bless Our Troops".

Sing "Bless Our Troops" by Teresa Jennings

1. We hope you enjoyed our show and learned something new today!

Many books in our library will tell you more about George Washington and the amazing Battle of Trenton. Please check them out!

2.   The ones used tonight in our script are:

Our Country's Founders by William J. Bennett, When Washington Crossed the Delaware by Lynne Cheney, George Did It by Suzanne Tripp Jurmain, and George Washington by James Cross Giblin (List books found in your Library).

3.   We leave you with a final thought from George Washington's own lips:

(Choose your favorite George Washington quote and say it here) or say
A man called Thomas Paine marched with the army and he came up with words to encourage the troops. "These are the times that try men's souls," he wrote. "The summer soldier and the sunshine patriot will, in this crisis, shrink from the service of their country; but he that stands it now, deserves the love and thanks of man and woman."

4.   Words to live by! Thank you for joining us in our salute to George Washington and all of our valiant veterans!

(ALL) Good Night! (Salute and Take a bow)
Play "Stars and Stripes Forever" as people exit.)

BOOK LIST

1. *A Color of His Own* by Leo Lionni
2. *Alexander and the Terrible, Horrible, No Good, Very Bad Day* by Judith Viorst
3. *Are You My Mother?* by P.D. Eastman
4. *Barnyard Banter* by Denise Fleming
5. *Barnyard Dance!* by Sandra Boynton
6. *Blueberries for Sal* by Robert McCloskey
7. *Brown Bear, Brown Bear, What Do You See?* by Bill Martin
8. *Click, Clack, Moo! Cows That Type* by Doreen Cronin and Betsy Lewin
9. *Commotion in the Ocean* by Giles Andreae
10. *Curious George* by H.A. and Margret Ray
11. *Dinosaurumpus!* by Tony Mitton
12. *Goodnight Moon* by Margaret Wise Brown
13. *Green Eggs and Ham* by Dr. Seuss
14. *Groovy Joe* by Eric Litwin
15. *Have You Seen My Cat?* by Eric Carle
16. *If You Give a Mouse a Cookie* by Laura Numeroff
17. *I Got the Rhythm* by Connie Schofiel-Morrison
18. *Love You Forever* by Robert Munsch, illustrated by Sheila McGraw
19. *Madeline* by Ludwig Bemelmans
20. *Make Way for Ducklings* by Robert McCloskey
21. *Monkey and Duck Quack Up!* by Jennifer Hamburg
22. *No, David!* by David Shannon
23. *Old Black Fly* by Jim Aylesworth
24. *Old MacDonald Had a Dragon* by Ken Baker
25. *Owl Moon* by Jane Yolen, illustrated by John Schoenherr
26. *Pete the Cat and His Four Groovy Buttons* by Eric Litwin
27. *Pete the Cat: I Love My White Shoes* by Eric Litwin
28. *SkippyJon Jones* by Judy Schachner
29. *Songs to Read* by Raffi
30. *Stand Tall, Molly Lou Melon* by Patty Lovell
31. *Stellaluna* by Janell Cannon
32. *Sylvester and the Magic Pebble* by William Steig
33. *The Crabfish* by John Feierabend
34. *The Gingerbread Man* by Jim Aylesworth
35. *The Giving Tree* by Shel Silverstein
36. *The Keeping Quilt* by Patricia Polacco
37. *The Little Engine That Could* by Watty Piper

38. *The Little Engine That Could* by Watty Piper, illustrated by George & Doris Hauman
39. *The Little House* by Virginia Lee Burton
40. *The Little Red Hen* by Jerry Pinkney
41. *The Mitten* by Jan Brett
42. *The Mysteries of Harris Burdick* by Chris Van Allsburg
43. *The Other Side* by Jacqueline Woodson, illustrated by E.B. Lewis
44. *The Polar Express* by Chris Van Allsburg
45. *The Pout-Pout Fish* by Deborah Diesen
46. *The Pout-Pout Fish Goes to School* by Deborah Diesen
47. *There Was An Old Lady Who Swallowed a Fly* by Simms Tabak
48. *The Snowy Day* by Ezra Jack Keats
49. *The Star Spangled Banner* by Peter Spier
50. *The Very Hungry Caterpillar* by Eric Carle
51. *Wemberly Worried* by Kevin Henkes
52. *Where the Wild Things Are* by Maurice Sendak

Additional Books

_____

_____

_____

_____

_____

_____

_____

_____

_____

_____

_____

_____

_____

_____

_____

_____

_____

ASSIGNMENT FORMS

CHAPTER 8: NOTE METHOD TEACHING SELF-ASSESSMENT

Name _____ Song _____

Fill out this form on your teaching experience, attach your one page summary using the guidelines below, and submit both to Blackboard.

Introduction/Engagement of Students	0	1	2	3	4		
Effective Use of Power Point	0	1	2	3	4	5	
Integration/Cross-Curricular	0	1	2	3	4		
Effective Use of Notation	0	1	2	3	4		
Effective Singing w/CD	0	1	2	3	4	5	
Effective Cueing	0	1	2	3	4		
Effective Use of Movement/Instruments	0	1	2	3	4	5	6
Specific Positive Feedback	0	1	2	3			
Addressing/Reteaching Student Learning	0	1	2	3			
Clear Directions and Leadership	0	1	2	3	4	5	6
Pacing/Energy Level	0	1	2				
Assessment	0	1	2				
Closure	0	1	2				
	T			/50			

Take some time to reflect on your teaching experience. Attach a one-page typed summary of your personal reflections which discusses the strengths and the areas needing improvement in your presentation. List and discuss at least three things which went well and at least three things which did not go as expected. Describe three ways you would change your teaching or the lesson plan if you had the opportunity to present this lesson to another class, and why would you make these changes?

CHAPTER 8: NOTE TEACHING TEACHER EVALUATION

Present this form with a copy of your lesson plan to the instructor prior to teaching your lesson

Name _____ Song _____

Introduction/Engagement of Students	0	1	2	3	4		
Effective Use of Power Point	0	1	2	3	4	5	
Integration/Cross-Curricular	0	1	2	3	4		
Effective Use of Notation	0	1	2	3	4		
Effective Singing w/CD	0	1	2	3	4	5	
Effective Cueing	0	1	2	3	4		
Effective Use of Movement/Instruments	0	1	2	3	4	5	6
Specific Positive Feedback	0	1	2	3			
Addressing/Reteaching Student Learning	0	1	2	3			
Clear Directions and Leadership	0	1	2	3	4	5	6
Pacing/Energy Level	0	1	2				
Assessment	0	1	2				
Closure	0	1	2				
	T			/50			

Name _____

The Young Person's Guide to the Orchestra

- Composed by Benjamin Britten

A Lesson About Orchestral Instruments and Timbre

Instructions: With a pair of good speakers or headphones, go to:

http://www.youtube.com/watch?v=4vbvhU22uAM&list=RD3HhTMJ2bek0

While watching this video of the Kölner Philharmonic's performance of Benjamin Britten's "The Young Person's Guide to the Orchestra," fill out the chart below.

Start Minute	Instrument(s) Featured	About the Instruments
00:05	All	*List the instruments of each instrument family, below.*
00:28	Woodwind Family	
00:51	Brass Family	
01:10	String Family	
01:27	Percussion Family	
01:43	All	*Describe the timbre of each instrument, below.*
02:05	Flute & Piccolo	
02:35	Oboe	
03:36	Clarinet	
04:20	Bassoon	

Thank you to Dr. Erin Hansen for sharing this music activity.

Name _____

Start Minute	Instrument(s) Featured	About the Instruments
05:11	Violin	
05:48	Viola	
06:46	Cello	
07:55	Bass	
08:54	Harp	
09:43	French Horn	
10:34	Trumpet	
11:01	Trombone (Tuba)	
11:17	Tuba (Trombone)	
12:16	Timpani	
12:31	Adds more percussion instruments	*Pick two percussion instruments that most caught your attention and describe their timbres.*
14:11	All	All of the instruments play the same theme (or a previous theme) in a fugue.

Final Questions:

1.What is your favorite part of the piece and why?

2.Which instrument's timbre do you find most pleasing and why?

CHAPTER 6: RUBRIC FOR LISTENING MAP ASSIGNMENT

Student _____

Recording quality. Length 1–2 minutes

Heading: Title and Composer

Educational Value of Music

Visual Large enough for all to see (chart, Power Point, Handout)

Visual Creativity, Artistic, Engaging, Colorful

Visual Accurate representation of music

Key defining symbols

Music Element (s)

Presentation Skills

CHAPTER 8: ROTE METHOD TEACHING SELF EVALUATION

Name _____ Song Title _____

Fill out this form on your teaching experience, attach your one page summary using the guidelines below, and submit both to Blackboard.

Song Introduction/Engagement of Students	0	1	2			
Appropriate Range, Starting Pitch	0	1	2			
Song Memorization	0	1	2			
Tuneful Singing	0	1	2	3	4	5
Correct Rhythm and Lyrics	0	1	2	3	4	5
Clear Directions and Leadership	0	1	2			
Rote Process	0	1	2	3	4	5
Effective Cue	0	1	2			
Specific Positive Feedback	0	1	2			
Addressing accuracy/re-teaching	0	1				
Closure	0	1				
Pacing/Energy Level	0	1				

Reflect on your teaching experience. Attach a one-page typed summary of your personal reflections which discusses the strengths and the areas needing improvement in your presentation. List and discuss at least 3 things which went well and at least three things which did not go as expected. Describe three ways you would change your teaching or the lesson plan if you had the opportunity to present this lesson to another class, and why would you make these changes?

CHAPTER 8: TEACHER ASSESSMENT FOR ROTE METHOD TEACHING

Name _____ Song Title _____

Directions: Present this form and a copy of your lesson plan to the instructor prior to teaching.

Song Introduction/Engagement of Students	0	1	2			
Appropriate Range, Starting Pitch	0	1	2			
Song Memorization	0	1	2			
Tuneful Singing	0	1	2	3	4	5
Correct Rhythm and Lyrics	0	1	2	3	4	5
Clear Directions and Leadership	0	1	2			
Rote Process	0	1	2	3	4	5
Effective Cue	0	1	2			
Specific Positive Feedback	0	1	2			
Addressing accuracy/re-teaching	0	1				
Closure	0	1				
Pacing/Energy Level	0	1				
T			/30			

CHAPTER 2: PICTURE BOOK ASSIGNMENT RUBRIC

Name _____ Book Title _____

I. Rhythmic Chant Rubric				
Direct pattern from book	0	1		
Addition of body percussion, movement or instruments	0	1	2	3
II. Presentation and Written Directions				
Clear explanation to the class, Effectiveness engaging students	0	1	2	3
Speaking skills, volume, easily understood, expression,				
Book facing class, eye contact	0	1	2	3
Format of lesson plan	0	1		
Information on the book. Title, Author, Publisher, ISBN#	0	1		
Easy to follow written directions	0	1	2	
Extensions	0	1		
Total score		/15		

INDEX

RHYTHM CARDS